Jackie
"The Joke Man"
Martling's

Disgustingly
Dirty Joke Book

Foreword by
Howard Stern

SIMON & SCHUSTER

Simon & Schuster

Rockefeller Center

1230 Avenue of the Americas

New York, NY 10020

Simon & Schuster and colophon are registered trademarks

of Simon & Schuster Inc.

Designed by Bonni Leon

Manufactured in the United States of America

1   3   5   7   9   10   8   6   4   2

Library of Congress Cataloging-in-Publication Data is available.

ISBN 0-684-84677-2

This book is dedicated to my lovely and talented wife, Nancy Sirianni, who has had these jokes coming at her a million different ways since 1974, still manages to laugh at them, and has not physically abused me yet. I love you, and I hope we're still married by the time someone reads this.

also . . .

A big hunk of warm must go out to my dear departed chum, Jake LeGrange, the Dutch salad man at Piping Rock Country Club where I was head busboy. For four years, I told him jokes nonstop, and he was absolutely unamused. It forced me to laugh at the jokes myself and develop the lunatic giggle that people know me by today.

Acknowledgments

I would like to thank my manager, Rory Rosegarten, for everything he keeps promising to do for me. I of course am indebted to Howard Stern for writing the foreword to this literary abomination, and for making me what I am today, a guy who writes joke books to pay his mortgage. Seriously, so much thanks.

I especially want to thank my parents, John and Dot, for the special combination of what they did and didn't do that made me the kind of guy who not only remembers every filthy joke, story, idea, rhyme, or saying he ever heard in his entire life, but has an unbridled obsession to share them with every human being he can, whether he's telling them at the bar or launching them into cyberspace. And much love to my sister Katie Dunn, who somehow endured the entire process and came through relatively unscathed. Lots of big hugs to Eileen Sidor, the Off Hour Rockers Inc. office manager/marriage counselor . . . please don't ever tell anyone what I'm really like.

I love Chris Bates for teaching me guitar in ninth grade so we could get laid and sneak into show business. Love to Bob Burford and Vinnie DiNapoli just for being my pals. I appreciate Robin Quivers, Fred Norris, Gary Dell' Abate, Stuttering John Melendez, and Scott Salem, from the world's greatest radio show, for listening to my crap since 1983, and I must aim a big wad of appreciation at K-Rock and CBS Radio and The E! Channel for that steady paycheck.

I want to thank my editor, Trish Todd, and my book designer, Bonni Leon. They both drew short straws and got to work on my project. A flipped bird must be aimed at my cover photographer, Brian Smale, who took such perverse delight in sticking real bars of soap into my mouth for two hours. I would thank my lawyers, Larry Shire and Mark Steverson, but I'm afraid I'd be billed for the time it would take them to read this fucking acknowledgment. Many thanks to Nerdland's Barry Jay and Lynn Harold for seeing to it that I occasionally had a functioning computer.

I'd thank my limo driver if I had one. Last but not least, thanks to anyone who ever went to any of my live shows, bought some of our JokeLand products, dialed (516) 922-WINE, or visited www. jokeland.com. I hope you enjoy the jokes . . . it's taken well over forty wild, soggy, and silly years to accumulate them.

Contents

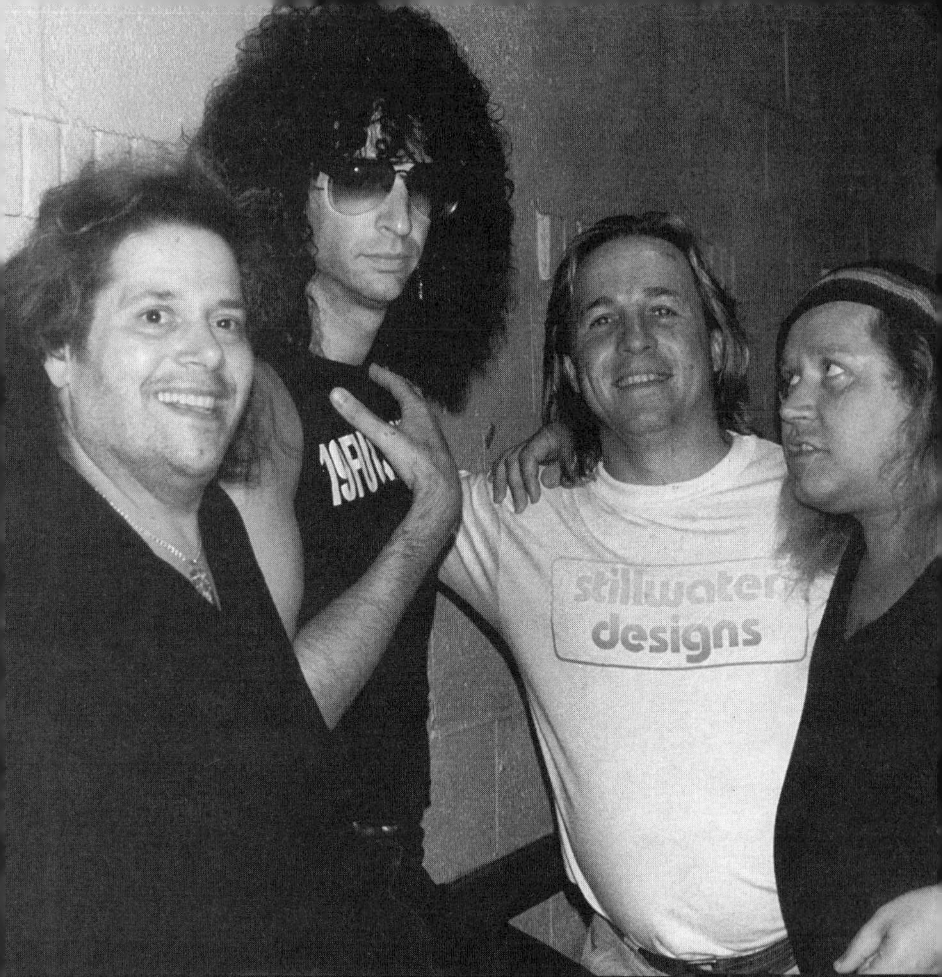
designs

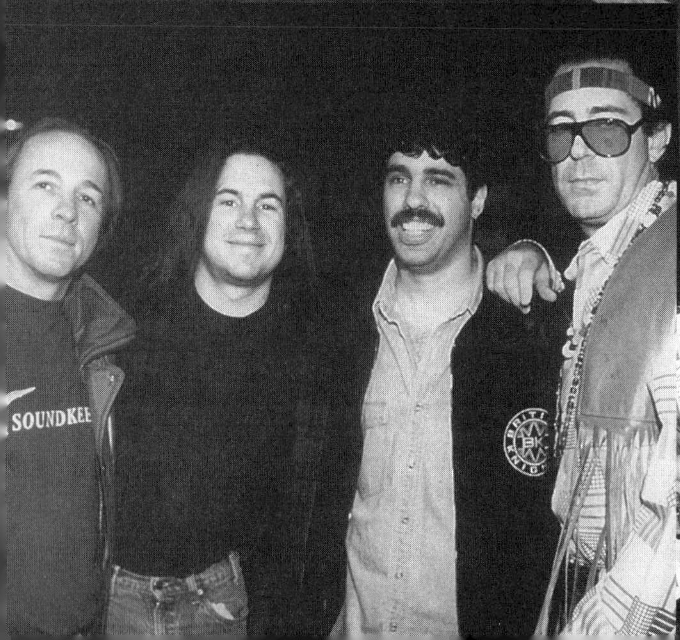

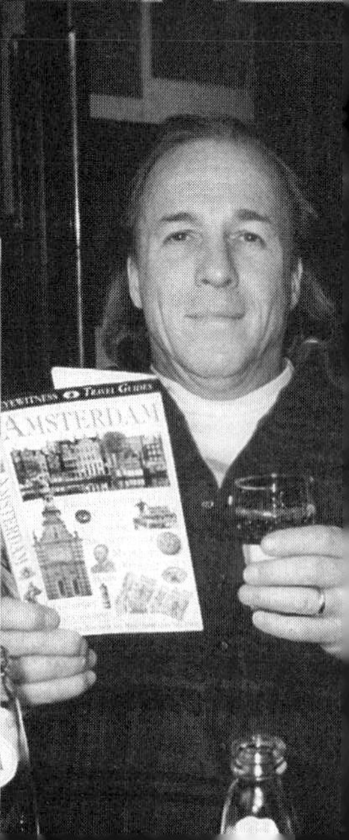
TRAVEL GUIDES
AMSTERDAM

Foreword by Howard Stern

Guess what? I won. No, not the lottery. I won the honor of writing the foreword to Jackie Martling's joke book. I must have an angel watching over me. In addition to having an undersized manhood, and a nose the size of a watermelon, I got chosen to write a piece on Jackie "The Joke Man" Martling.

You would think that the man chosen to write the foreword would know something about the contents of this book, but I really don't. Usually when you write a foreword they give you an advance copy and let you get familiar with the material. Jackie never gave me much information. He just grabbed ahold of me after the radio show a few months ago and mumbled something about book deal, the biggest break of his life, and the foreword . . . would you write it? I don't think he really wanted me to write this foreword, but the book company (Simon & Schuster) probably pressured him to somehow get me involved. It's called hedging their bet. They figure if you don't give a shit about Jackie, maybe you'll give a damn about my stupid intro. What morons these guys in publishing are. Like you're going to be stupid enough to buy this whole book just for a few measly pages from me. Any asshole with half a brain knows you can just stand in the bookstore and read my intro and then put the book back on the shelf. I read in the *New York Post* that Simon & Schuster paid Jackie five hundred thousand dollars for this book. If that is the case, they must be shitting in their collective pants and pressuring the bejesus out of Jackie to get me to write the stupid foreword. All I can tell you is that if Simon & Schuster paid him that much, then both Simon and his stupid partner Schuster should have their fucking heads examined. I've seen Jackie write joke books for pennies just so he could see his name on the cover of something. All I can say is Jackie sure saw these guys coming. Somebody better call the rape crisis center because I think Mr. Simon and Mr. Schuster just got bent over a chair and boned by an overweight wise guy. Personally, I refuse to believe that Jackie got anywhere close to that amount of money. It's the only way I'm going to be able to sleep at night.

Anyway, my guess is that the book is mostly wacky riddles and limericks or something. Jackie's whole life is wacky riddles and limericks. To tell you the truth, I don't care what the book is because chances are I'll be too busy to read it. Jackie has already written ten million joke books filled with riddles and limericks that I never read, and like all of Jackie's sad business stories they never sold, or they sold and the book company went bankrupt and screwed him out of his money.

Most people would be complimented to be asked to write the foreword to a book, but me, I'm annoyed. First of all, I hate writing. I especially hate writing when I'm not getting paid. Second, I hate when Jackie asks me to do something, because I really don't have the option of saying no. If I say no, he will pout and moan, and since he is my head writer he will probably take revenge on me and keep his best jokes to himself. Then his beautiful but annoying wife will fill Jackie's head with negative thoughts about me. In a sense, there's a gun to my head, so I just better do this and quit my bitching.

Usually when you write a foreword to someone's book you are very close to that person and you are most likely his or her best friend. I am not Jackie's best friend and I am certainly not close to him. In this case I am being given the honor of writing this foreword because I'm the most famous person that has met Jackie that is still willing to talk to him. Jackie knows Rodney Dangerfield, but Rodney no longer likes Jackie because Jackie owes Rodney two thousand dollars and refuses to pay back the loan. To call Jackie a welcher would be an understatement. As Jackie always says to me, "Hey, Rodney's got plenty of dough. What's he need with my lousy two grand?"

Jackie was friends with Eddie Murphy for ten minutes. Before Eddie Murphy got famous, he tried to befriend Jackie, but Jackie figured it was a good idea to blow off Eddie's friendship because "where the hell is this black kid going anyway? He can't do anything for me." So, here I am, the biggest celebrity in Jackie's life. My luck. I get to write the foreword when I could be outside by my pool on this beautiful June afternoon.

Now, don't let me mislead you. I love the Joke Man and I wish him well. I mean it. He's the funniest fucking guy and a hell of a lot of fun. We work together every day and have the best working relationship and chemistry a diss jockey and a joke man could ask for. The man can make me laugh, and he told me one of the sickest jokes I ever heard in my life. Jackie knows ten billion jokes. People tell me jokes all day and I can't remember any of them except for one that Jackie told me. Here it is:

A child molester is walking down the street with a young child, heading for the woods. The little boy says, "I'm afraid. It's dark, and I'm really scared." The child molester gives the little boy a disgusted look and says, "How do you think I feel? I have to walk home alone."

Now how can you not love a guy who tells you total garbage like that? Brilliant! Sick, but brilliant! Those words describe the Joke Man perfectly. Sick, brilliant. And, oh yes . . . charming. Jackie is charming. He's done incredibly charming things. Like having sex with amputees, shitting out of car windows, and he even pissed in his mother's face while he was trying to urinate in a beer bottle. Better yet, his grandmother caught him jerking off in the snow. I love that. The man has lived. The man has had life experience and I admire that. But that's all I know about the legendary Joke Man, the big outrageous stories. I realize sitting here that I don't know the small, intimate details of his life. Our relationship is so shallow that we never really communicate. I mean, every day I sit across from that lovable, wrinkled, weathered face that looks so much older than its forty-nine years, and I know so little about him. Does Jackie believe in God? Does Jackie read books? Does Jackie drink anything besides Bloody Marys? I mean, what the fuck is Jackie's favorite TV show? And has Jackie ever stuck his penis inside a prostitute's disease-ridden pussy? My God, I don't know the answers. I just don't know.

Jackie "The Joke Man" Martling's

Sure, I've visited his home and spent time with his sexy, horny wife, Nancy, but how well do I really know him? Walking through his abode and looking over his possessions didn't really tell me all that much about the man. Sure, I thought it was peculiar and incredibly vain that Jackie had hundreds of pictures of himself hanging on the walls of his dilapidated house, and I must admit it was rather disturbing seeing the stack of books his wife had lying around with titles like *How to Live with an Alcoholic.* I mean, what does that tell you about a guy? What, he likes a few cocktails? So the guy has a drinking problem and his wife can't deal with it. Jeez, that's just superficial stuff.

It's odd that I don't know that much about Jackie. What kind of man am I that I don't know squat about a guy who has written me some of my best material? I mean, sure I know that he has a horrible affliction on his feet called ten nail syndrome that left him with a yellowing, rotting fungus on his toenails that eventually led to all his nails being removed by a doctor that Jackie found in the *Pennysaver,* a free newspaper. Let's face it, that story alone tells you something about a guy. But it's just tip-of-the-iceberg stuff. Sure, I know a few stories about Jackie, like when he slept over some guy's house and he used the dude's toothbrush and thought that was perfectly fine, even though that toothbrush could have been covered in some kind of horrible infectious disease. He considered that normal behavior. You know what? You'll have to excuse me for a second, because I think I have to go throw up.

All right, I'm better now. Look, aside from Jackie's disgusting personal hygiene, I realized how little I knew about the Joke Man, and I decided to do a little research in an attempt to learn something about him. Here's everything I know after hours of exhaustive detective work. I worked hard on getting to know Jackie, and I really dug deep to find out the whole story. Maybe it's important to know something about Jackie, but most likely there is absolutely no good reason to know anything about Jackie. But I've got to write something.

So here goes . . . everything you want to know about Jackie.

John Coger (what's a Coger?) Martling, Jr., was born in Mineola, Long Island, a suburb of New York City, on February 14, 1948. Valentine's Day. He stands five feet seven and one-half inches tall and weighs 190 pounds. He comes from a long line of Republicans but is a registered Democrat, and he voted for both Clinton and Bush in previous elections. Jackie is a Methodist. Funny, but it never occurred to me that Jackie would be the slightest bit religious or hopeful of ever going to heaven after his history of screwing one-legged women and fat chicks only to dump them without explanation the next day. Jackie's held lots of jobs. He's worked as a caddie, a head busboy, a short-order cook, and a concrete form setter, and he managed a recording studio before starting a rock band and eventually becoming a stand-up comic.

His favorite films • *My Favorite Year* and *The Godfather* (I and II).
Favorite book • *Slaughterhouse-Five*. I know, that took me by
surprise as well.
Favorite TV shows • *The Larry Sanders Show* and *E.R.*

Out of all the celebrities we've ever had on the show, Jackie was most excited to meet Mickey Mantle. He thinks Pat Cooper is the funniest guest, and was most moved by the live in-studio performances of James Taylor.

Jackie "The Joke Man" Martling's

You would think that Jackie was a man of taste based on some of this information, but don't be fooled. It's Jackie's favorite song that disturbs me most. The brilliance of Hendrix, Zeppelin, and the Beatles is all wasted on the Martling eardrums, because Jackie thinks that something called "The Dutchman," written by some guy named Mike Smith and recorded by Steve Goodman, is the best song ever written. Now, that would probably explain why Jackie is a failed musician, and a song that he wrote, "The Pot Song," went straight to the bottom of the charts. Jackie's other song was a lot less frivolous. It was called "Cold Gold," and it was about his love of beer. Pretty heavy stuff. Starting to get a fuller picture of the author of this book? It ain't pretty, is it? It's goddamned sad is what it is, I'll tell you.

And who knew that Jackie had a nickname? Which of these would you guess is his?

> (A) Fuckface
>
> (B) Jewboy
>
> (C) The Chief

Well, if you said (C), the Chief, you'd be correct. The Chief? The Chief of what? Bayville, Long Island? Good grief.

Are you starting to know Jackie? Are you feeling closer to him? Or are you like me and you just realized that none of this information is useful or relevant?

Okay, so for those of you who are diehard fans of Jackie "the Joke Man," I'll quiz you some more.

Who in history would Jackie most like to meet?

  (A) Martin Luther King, Jr.

  (B) Lenny Bruce

  (C) Robert F. Kennedy

  (D) Percy Martling

Well, the pathetic answer is (D). Some loser named Percy Martling, whose only contribution to greatness was providing the sperm to produce Jackie's father.

Try another one.

Jackie was arrested for which offense?

  (A) Insufficient money for a speeding ticket in 1965

  (B) Drunk and disorderly in 1967

  (C) Caught with stolen goods in 1969

  (D) Driving while intoxicated in 1987

  (E) All of the above

Too easy, right? Of course it's (E), all of the above. God, that's depressing. Anybody feel like returning this book right now?

Look, the more I learn, the more disgusted I get, so let me wrap this up. Jackie likes blondes, if he could fuck one celebrity it would be Michelle Pfeiffer, and he drives a '93 Volvo station wagon. A Michigan State University grad with a degree in mechanical engineering, he has an IQ around 125, gets high two to three times a week, is pro-abortion, pro–death penalty (although he thinks it's barbaric), hates clothes shopping, and says his most charitable act was adopting a cat with cerebral palsy named Timmy. He's happiest swimming in Long Island Sound, likes Letterman better than Leno, doesn't care about the David

Lee Roth/Sammy Hagar controversy, and sleeps on his side with his asshole facing his wife. He wrote this book on a Pentium 166 using WordPerfect for Windows '95, claims his longest sex session occurred when he screwed a woman thirteen times in two days, is for school prayer (where the hell did that come from?), and ate lamb stew from our sponsor "the Soup Man" for breakfast this morning. His Jokeness prefers a neatly trimmed bush, scored 500 in English and 650 in math on his SATs, thinks Kevin Kelly, his former boss at the recording studio, is the smartest person he knows (even though it's really me and it pains him to admit it because he's so competitive), says a girl named Mary Zabelle, whom he never had sex with, is the sexiest woman he ever met besides his wife, and thinks Ronald Reagan, Louis Farrakhan, and Ted Kennedy are all assholes. Oh, and by the way—I didn't mean to keep you in suspense—the man drinks something besides Bloody Marys. It's Diet Coke. And he *has* put his penis inside the mouth of a prostitute (Juarez, Mexico, 1975).

There it is. That's everything I learned. And now, I leave it to you to decide what good my research has done. To quote that giant squid head Paul Harvey, "Now you know the rest of the story." So it is with great pleasure that I invite you to read a book by a whore-loving, dope-taking convict who loves the comedy of Red Skelton, Rodney Dangerfield, Johnny Carson, Redd Foxx, and the Marx Brothers. Sit back, relax, and enjoy the great comedy rhythms of a man who considers himself a gentle hippie, who wouldn't harm a fly, who claims that his most attractive feature is his ass, a hell of a great guy and friend, the Chief of God knows what, Jackie "the Joke Man" Martling.

—Howard Stern
June 1997

More Nerve Than Talent

Schmidlap is in a bus station men's room, and he has to take a dump. Now, I don't mean he's feeling rumblings in his stomach. I mean, he's got to *go*. He really has to pinch a loaf. The turtle is poking its head out and touching cotton. The corn is ready to ride the rocket.

He looks in the only stall, and there's not even a ring, just the bowl, with no ring on top. But he has to squeeze a weasel so bad, he doesn't care. So he's sitting on the bowl, and he's making a nice Carvel, when he looks and sees that there's no toilet paper. Now, who'd ever guess that a bus station bathroom with only one stall without a ring would have no paper? But it's too late, he's already laying cable. And he can't suck it back in, because it's already winding its way around the bowl.

He doesn't know what he's going to do, when he looks at the side of the stall and sees a little hole. Above it, it says, "Insert and finger will be cleaned by human lips."

He says, "Thank God."

He gets done, he wipes his ass with his finger, and then sticks it in the hole. A guy on the other side *smashes!* it with a hammer.

Schmidlap goes "*Oww!,*" yanks out his finger, sticks it in his mouth, and goes, "Mmmm."

How can you get a woman to make
a sound like a dolphin?
Flip her over and try to fuck her in the ass.
She'll go, "Eh—eh . . . eh-eh . . ."

The madam of a whorehouse is doing a bang-up business, so she decides to divide her reception area in half so she'll have another bedroom.

A carpenter puts up a wall, and then tells her, "That'll be fifteen hundred bucks, Miss."

She takes him by the hand, leads him into the new bedroom, takes off all of her clothes, and lies on the floor.

She says, "I don't have any cash, so I thought you might like to take it out in trade."

He gets down on the floor next to her, he puts his middle finger in her asshole and his thumb in her snatch and says, "All right, lady, give me my fifteen hundred bucks or I'm gonna rip out the partition."

Why did Disney World fail in Japan?
Nobody was tall enough to go on the good rides.

Collis walks into a store.

He says to the salesgirl, "I want to buy some toilet paper."

She says, "What color?"

He says, "Give me white. I'll color it myself."

What's the difference between making love to a girl *with* arms and making love to a girl *without* arms?
If you're making love to a girl without *arms and it pops out,* you *have to put it back in.*

Burford is going to the world's best whorehouse at 448 West Forty-eighth Street in Manhattan. He has a few beers, and by accident, he goes to *884* West *Eighty-fourth* Street, and it's a podiatrist's office.

He walks in and the nurse says, "Go behind the curtain and stick it out through the hole."

He does it.

She goes, "*Ahhh!* That's not a *foot.*"

He says, "I didn't know there was a minimum."

Why is it so hard for a woman to take a piss in the morning?
Did you ever try to peel apart a grilled cheese?

What's the difference between mayonnaise and sperm?
Mayonnaise doesn't hit the back of a girl's throat at thirty miles an hour.

There's a drunk at one end of a bar, and a woman in a tight low-cut dress at the other end of the bar. The woman is waving feverishly for the bartender, and she has an incredibly hairy armpit.

The drunk yells out, "Give me a drink, and give a drink to the ballerina at the other end."

The bartender says, "How do you know she's a ballerina?"

The drunk says, "Who else could get her leg up that high?"

It's Robin's first time at the gynecologist. She's up in the stirrups, and she's scared to death.

The gynecologist says, "You're nervous, aren't you?"

She says, "Yes. It's my first time at the gynecologist."

He says, "Would you like me to numb you down there?"

She says, "Please."

He sticks his nose in her twat and goes, "Num, num, num, num . . ."

A lady's walking down the street.

A guy says, "Hey, lady, there's a tampon hanging out of your mouth."

She says, "Fuck. What'd I do with my cigarette?"

A little kid comes running into the backyard.

He says, "Pop! Pop! Ma just got hit by a bus!"

His father says, "Son, you know my lips are chapped. Please don't make me smile."

Confucius say:

Schoolboy who fool around with schoolgirl during wrong period get caught red-handed.

Cathy hears that the local drugstore now features a mind-reading druggist, and she can't believe it. She goes down to the store, and there's a sign, right in the window, "Mind-Reading Druggist."

She walks in, and the druggist says to her, "You're here for suppositories."

She says, "Nope. I'm here for *tampons.*"

He says, "How much did I miss by?"

Jackie "The Joke Man" Martling's

Harris has a sore ass, so he goes to a proctologist.

The doctor examines him and says, "My God, how did your asshole get so stretched out?"

Harris says, "I got fucked by an elephant."

The doctor says, "Oh, come on, everybody knows elephants' dicks are *long,* but they're not that *wide.*"

Harris says, "He stuck his finger in first."

How can you tell if two lesbians are twins?
They lick alike.

Little old Mr. Ravelli is on his front stoop barbecuing a chicken on a manual rotisserie when a hippie comes walking along.

The hippie says, "Hey man . . . the music stopped, and your monkey's on fire."

Three ladies are in an obstetrician's waiting room.

The first lady says, "I'm going to have a girl, because I was on the bottom when we did it."

The second lady says, "I'm going to have a boy, because I was on the *top* when we did it."

The third lady says, "Fuck. I guess *I'm* gonna have a *puppy.*"

Did you hear about Tempura House?
It's a shelter for lightly battered women.

A cab driver picks up a nun.

He looks in the rearview mirror and says, "You know, Sister, I've always fantasized about being with a nun."

She says, "Yeah, you and everybody else. Are you Catholic?"

He says, "Yes, I am."

She says, "Pull over."

He pulls over, she gets in the front seat, and she gives him the best blow job he's ever had.

When she gets done, he feels a little guilty, and he says to her, "Sister, I have to tell you something. I'm not really Catholic."

She says, "Oh, yeah? Well, my name's Ralph, and I'm on my way to a costume party."

Jackie "The Joke Man" Martling's

Why does a dog lick his ass?
*Because he knows in five minutes he'll be
licking your face.*

Clooney and Riether are in a bar getting drunk.

Clooney says, "You know why I drink so much? Because my wife is so ugly."

Riether says, "Yeah? You think your wife's ugly? You should see my wife. She's a pig."

They keep drinking and arguing about who's wife is uglier, finally realizing the only way they're going to settle it is to see both of the women. So they go to Clooney's house, knock on the door, and his wife answers.

Riether says, "Sheesh, you got a point there. She's a show stopper. That face could send a train down a dirt road. But we still gotta see *my* wife."

When they get to Riether's house, they go into the living room, he pushes the couch, the chairs, and the table up against the wall, and then rolls up the rug. In the middle of the floor is a huge trap door.

He lifts it open and yells down, "Hey, Gertie! Come on up here!"

She says, "All right. Should I put the bag over my head?"

He says, "No, I don't want to *fuck* you. I just want to show you off."

Perna is boffing his old lady on the tile floor in the bathroom, right on the tile floor, he's boffing her . . .

He says, "Spread your legs! Spread your legs! Wider! *Wider!*"

She says, "What are you trying to *do?* Get your *balls* in?"

He says, "I'm trying to get 'em *out.*"

A teenage girl says to her father, "Daddy, I need a new dress for the prom."

He says, "You gotta give me a blow job."

She kneels down in front of him and puts his cock in her mouth.

She says, "Daddy, your dick tastes like shit."

He says, "Your brother had to rent a tuxedo."

A middle-aged divorcée wants to sleep with a black guy, she's dying to sleep with a black guy.

She goes to a bar, has a few drinks, meets a black guy, brings him home, brings him in the bedroom, takes off all her clothes, lies on the bed, spreads her legs, and says, "All right, pal, do what you do best."

So he grabs her TV and runs out the door.

What's the difference between looking for a lost golf ball
and Lady Godiva?
Looking for a lost golf ball is a hunt *on a* course.

Zuker is walking along the beach when he trips over a
bottle and a genie comes out.

The genie says, "Oh, thank you. I've been stuck in that
bottle for *centuries*. I'll tell you what . . . I'll give you one
wish. Anything you want."

Zuker pulls out a map of the Middle East, and he says,
"Could you bring peace to this part of the world?"

The genie says, "Gee, I don't know. They were fighting
there hundreds of years before I was even trapped in the
bottle. Have you got *another* wish?"

Zuker says, "Well . . . could you make it so once a
month my wife voluntarily gives me a blow job?"

The genie says, "Let me see that map again."

Why didn't Hitler drink vodka?
It made him mean.

How do you make a Jewish girl scream twice?
You fuck her in the ass and then wipe your dick on the drapes.

Mitchell's working at the lumberyard, pushing a tree through the buzz saw, and accidentally shears off all ten of his fingers. He goes to the emergency room.

The doctor says, "*Yuck!* Well, give me the fingers, and I'll see what I can do."

Mitchell says, "I haven't got the fingers."

The doctor says, "What do you *mean,* you haven't got the fingers? It's 1997. We've got microsurgery and all *kinds* of incredible techniques. I could have put them back on and made you like new. *Why* didn't you bring the fingers?"

Mitchell says, "Well, shit, Doc, I couldn't pick 'em up."

A Chinese couple's in bed.
The husband says, "I want-a sixty-nine."
His wife says, "Why you want beef and broccoli *now?*"

I hope you enjoyed this section.
And if you didn't, I bet that your dick is so small that you piss on your balls.

A Safe Distance from Genius

The year is 1958, and the ring announcer says, "Good evening, ladies and gentlemen, and welcome to Madison Square Garden and the World Heavyweight Boxing Championship. In this corner, weighing in at two-hundred-fifteen pounds, in the black trunks, it's the challenger from Sweden, Ingemar Johannsen. And in this corner, weighing in at two-hundred-five pounds, in the white trunks, the heavyweight champion of the world, from the United States of America, Floyd Paterson. Before we begin our bout, here to sing the National Anthem, we have America's sweetheart, the lovely Kate Smith."

A guy sitting ringside cups his hands around his mouth and yells, "Kate Smith? That fat pig? She sucked every cock on the East Coast."

The ring announcer says, "Nevertheless . . ."

How do you find a fat girl's snatch?
You flip through the folds until you smell shit,
and then go back one.

A Polish family is sitting in the living room.

The wife turns to the husband and says, "Let's send the kids out back to p-l-a-y, so we can fuck."

A lion is drinking from a puddle and his tail is up. A gorilla walks up behind him and slips him a Liberace. The gorilla takes off, and the lion takes off after him. The gorilla runs into a hunter's camp, jumps into a tent, puts on a safari outfit and a pith helmet, grabs a copy of the *Johannesburg Times,* sits down, and starts to read.

The lion runs into the camp, sticks his head into the tent, and roars, "*Arrgg!* Did a gorilla come through here?"

The gorilla says, "You mean the one that fucked the lion in the ass?"

The lion says, "My *God!* You mean it's in the *paper* already?"

A girl goes the doctor's office.
She says, "Doc, I need some contradiction."
He says, "You're ignorant."
She says, "Yep. Three months."

A seventy-five-year-old guy whose hair is completely white marries a twenty-two-year-old girl, and she gets pregnant.

Nine months later, he walks into the maternity ward and says to the nurse, "Well, how'd I do?"

The nurse says, "She had twins."

He says, "Heh, heh, heh. Well, I guess that goes to show, that even if there's snow on the roof, there can still be fire in the furnace."

She says, "Yeah? Well, then you'd better change filters. Both of the babies are black."

How can you tell the Polish girl on the nude beach?
*She's the one with the tampon string hanging
out of her asshole.*

Uchwat is fucking his wife in the ass for the first time.
She says, *"Ouch! That hurts!"*
He says, "No, it doesn't. It feels great."

A guy with three eyes, no arms, and one leg is hitchhiking.

A British guy pulls over, rolls down the window, and says, "Aye, aye, aye! You look 'armless! 'op in!"

What does it mean when two lesbians make love?
It doesn't mean dick.

A girl's on the witness stand.

The judge says, "What happened?"

She says, "I was walking down the sidewalk, when he grabbed me, dragged me into an alley, ripped off my dress, pulled down my panties, and bent me over a garbage can. I . . . I don't even remember what happened next."

The judge says, "Make something up! *Make something up!*"

What's the difference between a New York City
taxi driver and an elephant?
*The elephant has the trunk in the front and the
asshole in the back.*

Did you hear about the gay cannibal?
He blew lunch.

A couple gets married. Twenty years later, they're in the same hotel, in the same room, on the same bed.

She says, "Harry, what were you thinking twenty years ago on this night?"

He says, "I was thinking I'd like to fuck your brains out."

She says, "What are you thinking now?"

He says, "I think I did it."

Two guys are in a foxhole in Vietnam when one guy says, "I'm so horny, I can't stand it."

He jumps out of the foxhole and takes off. He comes back an hour later with a big grin on his face.

He says, "Man, it was great. Gook broad. What a body. I fucked her, fucked her in the ass, came on her tits . . . "

The other guy says, "Why didn't you get a blow job?"

He says, "I couldn't find her head."

The teacher says to the Polish high school girl, "What's the capital of Wisconsin?"

She says, "W."

Weir stops at a motel and there's a sign over the toilet that says, "Don't put anything but paper in this bowl."

So he shits on the floor.

Mrs. Stuart goes to a brand new gynecologist.

As he's examining her, he says, "Mrs. Stuart, that is the *hugest* vagina I have *ever,* ever seen."

When she gets home, she decides to have a look for herself, so she takes a big mirror down off the wall, puts it on the floor, takes off all of her clothes, stands on the mirror, spreads her legs, and looks down. Just then, her husband walks in early from work.

He says, "What the hell are you doing?"

She says, "Umm . . . I'm just exercising."

He says, "Well, be careful not to fall in the hole."

Did you hear about the Polish guy who bought
a toilet brush?
Two weeks later, he went back to paper.

McKenna is sitting at the bar jerking his meat.

The bartender says, "Look, Mac, you've got to get out of here."

McKenna says, "Are you kiddin'? I can't leave. I can't *walk.* I'm so drunk, I don't even know who I'm fuckin'."

Why did God give Italians arms?
So their fingers wouldn't smell like their armpits.

What do you say to a girl with no arms and no legs?
"Nice tits."

Favale goes to the doctor and says, "Doc, please help me. My wife and I can never come at the same time."

The doctor says, "It's easy. Put a gun loaded with blanks under your bed. The next time you're about to come, shoot the gun. She'll flood."

The next day Favale walks into the doctor's office looking really ragged.

The doctor says, "Well, did you try it?"

Favale says, "Yep."

The doctor says, "What happened?"

Favale says, "She bit off my cock, pissed in my face, and hasn't spoken to me since."

How is a Mexican like a cue ball?
The harder you hit 'em, the more English they pick up.

Hal is petrified of girls, so he asks his friend Lenny how he meets so many nice chicks.

Lenny says, "I have a surefire method to feel them out. I go up behind a girl and whisper, 'Tickle your ass with a feather?' And when she of course turns around and asks what I said, I say, 'Particularly nice weather.' If she smiles or laughs, I know she has a sense of humor, we chat, and it all follows naturally. Try it."

The next night, nervous but desperate, Hal goes to a very crowded bar, and sits in the corner, stewing, nursing a drink, getting more uptight every second.

Finally, he walks up behind the nicest girl in the place, and after a few minutes of stammering, blurts out so everybody can hear, "Stick my finger in your ass?"

She turns and says, *"What?"*

He says, "Look at the fucking rain."

What's the difference between Jesus
and a picture of Jesus?
It only takes one nail to hang up a picture of Jesus.

What's the difference between a straight
guy and a gay guy?
*When something goes up a straight guy's ass,
there's usually a fingernail on it.*

The Mother Superior is out bicycling with a dozen nuns and the nuns are giggling, and chuckling, and carrying on.

The Mother Superior says, "Calm down now, girls, or I'm going to have to put the seats back on those bikes."

Wolanin gets on a bus in San Francisco and suddenly realizes the entire bus is loaded with homos.

He says to the driver, "Hey! I want to get off!"

The driver says, "Don't worry."

Where would you find a turtle with no legs?
Right where you left him.

Halvangis comes home from work to find his wife in the kitchen on all fours, wearing nothing but her bathrobe, scrubbing the kitchen floor. He comes up behind her, lifts up her robe, fucks her fast and hard doggie-style, and then *smacks* her in the head.

She says, "I let you do something so nice like that . . . what'd you *hit* me for?"

He says, "For not looking to see who it was."

What's the difference between being a dentist
and being a gynecologist?
The teeth.

Two gynecologists meet at lunch.

The first one says, "I had a patient this morning with a clit like a dill pickle."

The second one says, "That *big* or that *green?*"

The first one says, "That *sour.*"

A drunk stumbles into a confessional.

The priest hears him come in, but then he doesn't hear anything, so the priest knocks on the wall.

The drunk says, "Forget it, buddy, there's no paper in this one, either."

What's the difference between shooting arrows
at lovers and Kathy Lee Gifford?
Shooting arrows at lovers is a Cupid stunt.

I hope you enjoyed this section.
*If you didn't, why don't you go rent
yourself out as a laxative . . . you're
irritating the shit out of me.*

Hoof
Hearted?
Ice Melted.

Berman works a new job on Thursday and Friday.

On Monday he calls in and says, "I can't come in today. I'm sick."

He works the rest of the week, but the following Monday he calls in and says, "I can't come in today. I'm sick."

The boss asks the foreman about him, and the foreman says, "He's great. He does the work of two men. We need him."

So the next day the boss calls Berman into his office, and says, "You seem to have a problem getting to work on Mondays. You're a good worker and I'd hate to fire you. What's the problem? Anything we can help you with? Drugs? Alcohol?"

Berman says, "No, I don't drink or do drugs. But my brother-in-law drinks every weekend, and then beats up my sister. So every Monday morning, I go over to make sure she's all right. She puts her head on my shoulder and cries, one thing leads to another, and the next thing you know, I'm fucking her."

The boss says, "You fuck your *sister?*"

Berman says, "Hey, I told you I was *sick.*"

How about the two maggots who were making love in dead Ernest?

A winded young lass named Voghill,
Sat down to rest on a molehill . . .
The resident mole,
Stuck his nose in her hole.
Miss Voghill's okay, but the mole's ill.

Quasimodo is in the kitchen when his mother walks in carrying a wok.

He grunts, "Oh, good. I love Chinese food."

His mother says, "What are you talking about, Chinese food? I'm gonna use this thing to iron your shirts."

How can you tell the Irish guy in
the hospital ward?
*He's the one blowing the foam
off of his bedpan.*

Van der Leun goes on a date with an Oriental girl and gets real drunk.

He mumbles, "You know why I asked you out on a date? Because I wanted to find out, once and for all, if it really goes from side to side instead of up and down."

She says, "Whatsa difference? Whataya, play the harmonica or something?"

Why do they put shit on the altar at Italian weddings?
To keep the flies off the bride.

What did Davy Crockett say at the Alamo?
"Where the fuck did all these landscapers come from?"

Did you hear about the new morning-after pill for men?
It changes their blood type.

Broder has tried to get his wife to blow him his entire married life, but she's never given in. He's tried again and again, but she's always said no. He's begged, and pleaded, but she's always insisted that she'd rather die a horrible, twisted death than ever do it.

One night, the argument gets very heated, and after hours of screaming, yelling, crying, ranting and raving, she finally gives in and agrees that he deserves a little variety. She takes his peter in her hand, and then slowly starts to put it in her mouth. Just as she gets her lips over the head, the phone rings, and Broder answers it.

He says, "Hello? Yeah, she's home."

He looks down at her and says, "It's for you, cocksucker."

A guy goes into a dentist's office, sits down in the chair, and takes out his dick.

The dentist says, "What are you *doing?* I'm a *dentist.*"

The guy says, "There's a *tooth* in there."

Professor Kelly goes to bed with his wife. He's not that tired, so he decides to stay awake and read while she goes to sleep. Every once in a while, he reaches over and tickles her pussy.

After a few minutes, she says, "Kelly, will you *stop* that? Will you stop reaching over and *teasing* me like that?"

He says, "I'm not *teasing* you. I'm wetting my fingers so I can turn the page."

How can you tell when the Orientals have moved into your neighborhood?
The Mexicans *get car insurance.*

Nancy goes to the gynecologist.

She says, "Doctor, I'm freaking out. My pee is coming out in four streams."

He examines her and starts to giggle.

She says, "It's not funny. My pee is coming out in four streams."

He says, "It won't anymore. I took the trouser button out of there."

Did you hear about the skinny guy who went to Alaska?
He came home a husky fucker.

How is climbing a mountain like getting a blow job from
Whoopie Goldberg?
Don't ever look down.

A couple gets married. Forty years later, they're in the same hotel, in the same room. She takes off her clothes, lies down on the bed, spreads her legs . . . and he starts to cry.

She says, "What's the matter?"

He says, "Forty years ago I couldn't wait to eat it, and now it looks like it can't wait to eat *me.*"

When do you know you're really ugly?
Dogs hump your leg with their eyes closed.

Leeds is drinking all afternoon and suddenly pukes all over his shirt.

He slobbers, "My wife is gonna kill me."

The bartender says, "Put a twenty-dollar bill in your top pocket and tell your wife that a drunk threw up on you and then gave you the twenty bucks to get it cleaned."

He agrees it's a great idea. When he gets home, he walks in, tells her the story, and hands her the money.

She says, "But there's *forty* dollars here."

He says, "Yeah, he shit in my pants, too."

Why don't Jewish girls swallow?
They want to be the spitting images of their mothers.

A priest is teaching a nun how to swim.

She says, "Father, will I really sink if you take your finger out?"

It's Ratcliffe's first day in the car pool. They honk the horn in front of his house, and he comes running out. He gets about halfway down the walk when he hears the sound of his wife's foot tapping on the porch. He turns around, and there she is, scowling at him. He runs back to the steps, spreads her bathrobe, bends over, kisses her on the snatch, runs back down the walk, and hops in the car.

They ride in silence for a few minutes, until Sack, the driver, can't stand it, and says, "Ratcliffe, I don't mean to pry, but my curiosity is *killing* me. Why did you kiss her down *there?*"

Ratcliffe says, "Man, you should *smell* her breath in the morning."

When I die, I want to go like my grandfather. Peacefully, in his sleep.

Not screaming, like his passengers.

Why do men pay more than women for car insurance?
Because women don't get blow jobs while they're driving.

Shapiro meets a girl on the street.

He says, "Come on, babe, let's go in the alleyway and get it on, I've got fifteen bucks."

She says, "*Fifteen bucks?* You're crazy. For fifteen bucks, I'll let you *look* at it."

He says, "All right."

They go into the alleyway, she pulls down her pants, and he gets down on his knees. But he can't see anything, because it's too dark, so he gets out his lighter.

He lights his lighter, and he says, "My God, your pubic hair . . . it's so curly, and thick . . . it's *beautiful.*"

She says, "Thank you."

He says, "You mind if I ask you a personal question?"

She says, "Go ahead."

He says, "Can you *pee* through all that hair?"

She says, "Of course."

He says, "Well, you'd better start. You're on fire."

Two Polish guys go hunting. They take two guns and three dogs.

A half hour later they come back . . . for more dogs.

What's the difference between menstrual fluid and sand?
You can't gargle with sand.

Why do Jews buy generic rubbers?
They're cheap fuckers.

Why can't Helen Keller drive?
She's a woman.

A college kid says to his friend, "I fucked my roommate in the ass last night."

His friend says, "No shit?"

He says, "A little."

How can you tell if a girl is a redneck?
She can suck a dick and chew tobacco
at the same time, and know what to spit
and what to swallow.

I hope you enjoyed this section.
If you didn't, remind me to call your
parents if I ever need the blueprints
to build myself an asshole.

Use Your Finger!

It's very early one morning, and two bums are walking along in a park.

The first bum says, "Man, I gotta take a dump."

The other bum says, "Well, do it right here. There's nobody around, it's early."

The first bum says, "You think so? Right here?"

The other bum says, "Yeah."

So he figures he will, because it helps the joke. He pulls down his pants and squats down.

All of a sudden, he hears, "Clop clop clop . . . clop clop clop."

He listens again, and he hears, "Clop clop clop . . . clop clop clop."

He says, "Hey, man, you hear that?"

The other bum says, "Hear what?"

He says, "Listen."

"Clop clop clop . . . clop clop clop."

The second bum says, "Man, how long's it been since you ate?"

The first bum says, "About three weeks."

The second bum says, "That's your asshole nibbling on the grass."

Why did God make gold chains?
To remind the Italians where to stop shaving.

Thomas goes to the zoo to feed the monkeys. He throws a monkey a peanut, the monkey picks it up, sticks it in his rear end, pulls it out, and eats it.

Thomas goes, *"Yuk!"*

He throws the monkey another peanut. The monkey picks it up, sticks it in his rear end, pulls it out, and eats it.

Thomas goes, *"Yuk!"*

He goes to the zookeeper, and he says, "Man, that is one very *stupid* monkey."

The zookeeper says, "No, that's a very *smart* monkey. Last week, somebody threw him a big peach, and he ate it, and he couldn't pass the pit. So now he *measures* everything first."

A black guy is standing in front of a brand-new Cadillac when a salesman walks up and says, "Thinking about buying a Cadillac?"

The black guy says, "No, I *am* buying a Cadillac. I'm *thinkin'* about *pussy.*"

Why do Italian organ grinders always have a monkey with them?
Somebody has to do the bookkeeping.

Mrs. Bandlow says to her husband, "I had the strangest dream last night. It was Christmas, and our tree was decorated with all kinds of penises. White ones, black ones, circumsized and uncircumsized, big and small. And on the top of the tree was the perfect penis."

Bandlow says, "I bet that one was mine."

She says, "Sorry, honey, it wasn't."

He says, "You know, it's weird, but I had almost the same dream. A Christmas tree decorated with pussies . . . shaven and unshaven, thin and thick lips, scented and unscented . . . and on the top of the tree was the perfect pussy."

She says, "I suppose the one on the top was mine?"

He says, "Nope. *Yours* was holding up the tree."

Chester walks into Marshall Dillon's office with a huge boner.

The Marshall says, "For Christ's sakes, Chester, go out in the barn and stick that thing in a shovelful of horseshit."

Chester walks into the barn with this huge hard-on, and Miss Kitty is lying in the hay playing with herself. She takes one look at Chester, spreads her legs, and says, "Put it in there, Chester."

He says, "The whole shovelful?"

Mr. and Mrs. Nearier come before the judge for their divorce hearing.

The judge says, "What are the grounds?"

Mrs. Nearier says, "Cruel and inhuman punishment. He tied me to the bed and then forced me to sing the National Anthem while he pissed all over me."

The judge says, "My God, that's horrible."

She says, "Yeah. He *knows* how much I hate that fucking song."

Three guys and a girl are marooned on a desert island. After one week, the girl is so ashamed of what she's doing, she kills herself.

After *another* week, the *guys* are so ashamed of what they're doing, they *bury* her.

After *another* week, they're so ashamed of what they're doing, they dig her up again.

What's the significance of that little red dot in
the middle of an Indian woman's forehead?
It means "coffee's ready."

Morell walks into a doctor's office and sticks out his nine-inch tongue.

The *nurse* goes, "Ahh . . ."

Two worms live together on a golf course.

The first worm says, "What kind of day is it?"

The other worm says, "You know, I don't know, but I was thinking of going up and checking it out."

The first worm says, "That's a good idea. Why don't you do that."

So the second worm starts on his way up through the dirt. At the same time, two lady golfers are walking along the fairway.

The first one says, "Jeez, I gotta whiz."

Her friend says, "Hey, it's real early. There's nobody else here on the course. Do it right here. Nobody'll know."

The first lady says, "You think so? Right here?"

Her friend says, "Yeah."

She pulls down her skivvies, lifts up her little golf dress, she squats, and she's just about to commence when the worm pokes his head up out of the grass right below her. She lets fly, and forget it, he gets drenched. He's dripping wet as he goes back down through the dirt. He comes up to the first worm, and he's soaking wet.

The first worm looks at him and says, "Oh, it's raining, eh?"

The second worm says, "Not only is it raining, it's raining so hard the birds are building their nests upside-down."

Lydia is black and blue, and she stands before the judge crying.

She says, "Your Honor, he gets up every morning and starts knocking me around the bedroom. He hits me on the head with his fist, and sometimes whacks me with his belt. If I don't fix his meals just right, he hits me with a pot or pan. If I dare to say anything back to him, he throws a beer bottle at me. You've got to put him in jail, or he's gonna kill me."

The judge turns to her boyfriend and says, "Well, what have you got to say for yourself?"

Lydia's boyfriend says, "You can't believe a word she says, your Honor. She's obviously punch drunk."

Lewis wants to join the Big Dick club.

He goes down to the local chapter and says to the receptionist, "I want to join."

She says, "How long is it?"

He says, "Eighteen inches."

She goes into such a hysterical laughing fit that he turns around and runs out, totally embarrassed. On his way, he passes a guy sweeping.

Lewis says, "I can't believe I told the receptionist I've got eighteen inches and she laughed in my face."

The sweeper says, "Listen, pal, there's a lot of competition here. See that lump in my sock? I'm only the janitor."

What's the difference between driving in the fog
and eating pussy?
*When you're driving in the fog, you can't see the
asshole in front of you.*

Heidi stumbles into a bar.

She says, "Beertender, give me a dribble martoonie,
and put a pickle in it."

He gives it to her, and she drinks it down.

She says, "Beertender, give me another dribble martoonie, and put a pickle in it."

He gives it to her, and she drinks it down.

She says, "Beertender, give me another dribble martoonie, and you better put *two* pickles in it, becau . . .
because I've got heartburn."

The bartender says, "Look, lady . . . it's not *beertender*,
it's *bartender*. It's not a *martoonie,* it's a *martini.* It's not a
dribble, it's a *double.* That's not a *pickle,* it's an *onion.* And
you haven't got heartburn, you've got your left tit in the ash-
tray."

Why don't Italians have zits?
They slide off.

Jackie "The Joke Man" Martling's

Did you hear about the Polish girl who burnt her
twat on the Fourth of July?
She lit the fuse to her tampon.

What do you get when you cross a hooker with a piranha?
Your last blow job.

Did you hear about the Chinese couple that had
a black baby?
They named him "Sum Ting Wong."

I hope you enjoyed this section.
*If you didn't, why don't you go get
yourself a glass belly button? Then,
when your head was this far up
your ass, you could look out and see
what the rest of us are doing.*

Strangers
in My Mouth

Vasillas goes into a barber shop, sits down in the chair, the barber cuts his hair, and after he gets done, as Vasillas gets up and is taking out his money, the barber goes over and takes a leak in the corner of the barber shop. The barber finishes and comes back.

As Vasillas hands him a twenty-dollar bill, he says, "Listen, it's . . . it's none of my business, but *why* . . . why would you take a piss in the corner of your own barber shop?"

The barber says, "Hey, my lease is up in two weeks. Do I care?"

The barber goes over to the cash register, rings up the haircut, comes back with Vasillas' change, and Vasillas is standing there taking a shit on the floor.

The barber says, "What are you doing?"

Vasillas says, "Well, fuck, I'm leaving *now.*"

Why do nipples have all those little
bumps around them?
It's braille for "lick here."

An old guy goes to the doctor.

The doctor examines him and says, "You've got cancer and Alzheimer's."

He says, "Thank God I haven't got cancer."

Jackie "The Joke Man" Martling's

Bales starts working in a lumber camp.

The boss says, "We work twelve hours a day, we eat two meals a day, lights out at ten-thirty, and you can put your dick in the barrel over there for a blow job any day but Thursday."

Bales says, "Why not Thursday?"

The boss says, "Because Thursday is your turn in the barrel."

Forman walks into a bar with a huge bruise on his forehead.

The bartender says, "What the hell happened to you?"

He says, "I was in the backyard fucking my wife doggie style when she ran under the house."

How about the Polish girl who had all of her teeth pulled, so she'd have more gum to chew?

Gail goes to the doctor with her knees all cut up.

The doctor says, "What happened to your knees?"

She says, "It's from making love doggie style."

He says, "Don't you know any other position besides doggie style?"

She says, "Yeah, but my doggie don't."

A little old lady walks into a luncheonette, sits down, and says, "I'd like a hamburger."

The big, fat, disgusting guy behind the counter yells, *"Bur-ger."*

The cook, who's bigger and fatter and even *more* disgusting, yells back, *"One bur-ger."*

He grabs a big hunk of chopped meat, puts it in his bare armpit, pumps his arm to flatten it, and throws it on the grill.

She looks at the guy behind the counter and says, "I think that's the most dis*gusting* thing I've ever seen in my *entire life.*"

He says, "Yeah, lady? You should be here in the morning when he makes the doughnuts."

Guys, you know you've been married too long
when the only reason you go down on it is because
it doesn't talk back.

When is it okay to spit in an Italian girl's face?
When her mustache is on fire.

Why don't women have any brains?
Because they don't have a dick to carry them around in.

Cooper walks into a doctor's office and says, "Doc, you gotta help me. I've got a constant erection. At first it was fun, but then it became painful and embarrassing."

While the doctor's examining him, a bug jumps off his dick and his boner goes right down.

Cooper says, "Gee, Doc, that's great. How much do I owe you?"

The doctor says, "Help me find that bug and you don't owe me anything."

A couple's in the living room.

He says, "You're dry tonight."

She says, "You're licking the rug."

Two ladies are in the veterinarian's waiting room.

The first one says to the second one, "What are you doing here?"

She says, "My kitty keeps going into the living room and scratching up the furniture, so I'm having her declawed. What about you?"

The second one says, "Oh, it's my puppy. Every time I bend over, he humps me in my ass."

The first one says, "Oh, so you're having him neutered?"

The second one says, "No, I'm having *him* declawed, too."

Who's the world's greatest athlete?
A guy who finishes first and third in
a masturbation contest.

Jackie "The Joke Man" Martling's

A slug is sexually assaulted by two turtles, and the slug's on the witness stand.

The judge says, "All right, which one of them went first?"

The slug says, "I don't know, your Honor. Everything happened so *fast*."

The Cantors are driving along when they see a wounded skunk on the side of the road. They stop, Mrs. Cantor gets out, picks it up, and brings it into the car.

She says, "Look, it's shivering. It must be cold. What should I do?"

He says, "Put it between your legs."

She says, "What about the smell?"

He says, "Hold its nose."

Grillo goes to visit his grandmother and takes one of his friends with him. While he's talking to his grandmother, his friend starts eating the peanuts on the coffee table, and he eats them all.

As they're leaving, his friend says to his grandmother, "Thanks for the peanuts."

She says, "Yeah, since I lost my dentures I can only suck the chocolate off 'em."

Did you hear about the blind skunk?
He fucked a piece of shit.

DePace buys a country house down South, and the day he's moving in, there's a knock on the door.

He answers, and a guy at the door says, "Hi, neighbor. Why don't you come on over Saturday night? Lots of eatin' an' drinkin' an' fightin' an' fuckin'."

DePace says, "Sounds good. What should I wear?"

The other guy says, "It don't much matter. It's just gonna be me and you."

Norris goes to pick up his blind date at her house, and when he gets there he finds out she has no arms and no legs. He's a good sport, so he picks her up, puts her in his car, and takes her to a movie. When the movie's over, he picks her up again and puts her back in the car.

She says, "Do you have any rope in the car?"

He says, "Rope? Why, yeah, I got some rope."

She says, "Do you know that big old oak with the real low limb down in the dark corner of the park?"

Norris says, "Yeah."

She says, "Why don't you take us there?"

When they get there, she has Norris get out the rope, undress her, and then she gives him explicit instructions how to use the rope to suspend her from the limb. And then, they proceed to have the wildest sex that Norris has ever had. When they're done, Norris drives her home, carries her inside, and puts her on the living room couch.

As he's leaving, her father grabs him by the arm and says, "Here, son," and goes to hand Norris five hundred dollars.

Norris says, "I can't take that, sir."

Her father says, "Please, son, take the money."

Norris says, "I can't, sir. You see . . . I . . . I had sex with your daughter."

Her father says, "Of course you did. But at least you didn't leave her hanging from that fucking tree."

Why did cavemen drag their women by the hair?
*Because if they dragged them by the feet, their twats
would've filled up with mud.*

Corson walks into a bar, sits down next to Trueson, and bets Trueson that he can bite his eye. Trueson takes the bet, Corson takes out his glass eye, and he bites it.

Then he bets Trueson he can bite his *other* eye. Trueson takes the bet, because he knows Corson isn't blind. Then Corson takes out his false teeth and bites his other eye.

A big, fat lady walks into a bar with a duck under her arm.

The bartender says, "Hey, where'd you get the pig?"

She says, "It's not a *pig,* it's a *duck.*"

He says, "I was talking to the *duck.*"

What would you call an Amish guy
with his hand in a horse's ass?
A mechanic.

Paterson walks up to a woman wearing a full-length fur.

He says, "Do you know how many animals had to die for that coat?"

She says, "Do you know how many animals I had to *fuck* for this coat?"

What would you call a female turtle?
A clitortoise.

Did you hear they came out with a new Selena doll?
Barbie and Ken needed a maid.

Why did God put a woman's two
holes so close together?
In case you miss.

Quinn is in a huge barroom brawl, and his jaw gets smashed up real bad. They wire it shut, so for a couple of weeks he'll have to be fed through his ass.

After a few days, he goes in to see his doctor, and the doctor says, "How are you feeling, Mr. Quinn?"

Quinn is bobbing up and down, bending at the knees, and he says, "Oh, I feel pretty good, Doc. Can't complain. You know me, I don't complain. Nope. No complaints."

The doctor says, "Well, is there a lot of pain where your jaw's wired shut?"

Quinn, still bobbing up and down, says, "No. No pain. Nope. I hardly even notice it. Hardly even notice it."

The doctor says, "Well, is it a big inconvenience being fed through your butt?"

Quinn, still bobbing up and down, says, "No. No, not at all. No inconvenience at all."

The doctor says, "Mr. Quinn, *why* are you bobbing up and down like that?"

He says, "I'm chewin' gum."

How do you circumcise a hillbilly?
Kick his sister in the chin.

Jackie "The Joke Man" Martling's

Stern goes into a luncheonette and orders a hamburger and a hot dog.

A few minutes later, the waitress puts a plate in front of him with an open bun on it, pulls a hamburger out from under her armpit, and tosses it on the bun.

Stern says, "What the hell was *that* all about?"

She says, "I was just keeping it warm for you."

He says, "Cancel my hot dog."

How can you tell one end of a worm from the other?
Put it in a bowl of flour and wait for it to fart.

I hope you enjoyed this section. *If you didn't, why don't you go stick your brain up an ant's ass and listen to it roll around like a BB in a boxcar.*

RAINBOW!

Lipstick on My Dipstick

Hoffmann is buying a used motorcycle from his cousin.

He says, "My God, it's so shiny, it's like *new*. What's your secret?"

His cousin says, "Well, any time it's about to rain, I coat the chrome with a little Vaseline so it won't tarnish. In fact, I won't be needing this any more, here, take my tube."

Hoffmann goes to pick up his girlfriend on the motorcycle. They're going to her parents' house for dinner and he's going to meet them for the very first time.

On the way she says to him, "Listen, I have to tell you something. My family's a little strange. You can't talk during dinner. If you talk during dinner, you have to do the dishes."

He thinks, "All right."

When they go into her parents' house, not only in the kitchen, but in the dining room, the living room, on the stairs, the back porch, *everywhere,* there are piles and piles of dirty dishes. They haven't done the dishes in *months.* They sit down to eat, and the whole meal, nobody talks. During dessert, Hoffmann is getting a little horny, and he figures nobody is going to say anything, so he grabs his girlfriend and *pops!* her right there on the dining room table.

Nobody says nothing.

He's still a little horny, and her mother is kind of cute, so he figures, what the hell. He throws her mother up on the table and starts to do *her.* He's just about done with her when he looks out the window and sees it's starting to rain on his motorcycle. He reaches into his pocket and takes out the tube of Vaseline.

Her father jumps up and says, "All right, all right, I'll do the fucking dishes."

Goodstein goes on a date, and puts in his finger.

She says, "Put in another finger."

He says, "What do you wanna do? *Whistle?*"

A kid says, "Pop, what's a vagina look like?"

His father says, "Son, before sex, a vagina looks like a rose, with pink, velvety petals, and the aroma of perfume."

The kid says, "What about *after* sex?"

His father says, "Have you ever seen a bulldog eating mayonnaise?"

Why don't they put Al Sharpton on a stamp?

Nobody would know which side to spit on.

What would you call it when an Italian has
one arm shorter than the other?
A speech impediment.

How do you know if you've got a great sperm count?
She has to chew before she swallows.

Dan Quayle calls home from the Reserves.

He says, "Pop, yesterday they took us skydiving."

His father says, "What happened?"

He says, "Well, I was last, and I told the sergeant I couldn't do it, that I was too scared. And he said to me, 'Well, son, I'm gay, and there's only *one* way you're getting out of it.'"

His father says, "Did you jump?"

He says, "A little at first."

A middle-aged guy and his date are in the movies making out hot and heavy when his toupee slides off.

As he's groping around for it, his hand goes between her legs, up her skirt, and lands on her twat.

She says, "That's *it!* That's *it!*"

He says, "It can't be. I part mine on the side."

A little mouse is running along when an eagle swoops down, swallows him, and then takes off again.

A few minutes later the mouse *pops!* his head out of the eagle's ass.

He says, "How high up are we?"

The eagle says, "About a mile."

The mouse says, "You wouldn't *shit* me, wouldja?"

Jack calls a girl for a date.

She says, "But, Jack, I've got my menstrual cycle."

He says, "So I'll come over on my moped."

Walters is standing outside a condo in Miami Beach when all of a sudden he hears, "Hello, handsome."

He looks up and sees a middle-aged woman, naked from the waist up, hanging out of a window. And she's got beautiful jugs.

She says, "Come on up. 14B."

Needless to say, he runs into the hotel, goes up in the elevator, runs down the hall to 14B, and knocks on the door. She opens the door, pulls him in, and closes the door. She's stark naked, except for bikini panties. He can't believe it. She leads him into the living room, not saying a word. She unbuckles his belt, pulls down his zipper, undoes his pants, and pulls them down to his ankles. She pulls his T-shirt up to his chest, and pulls down his underpants. He's got a boner like you write home about.

She cups his hard-on in her hand, strokes it a few times, and then she starts *smacking!* it, and says, "Don't-you-ever-park-in-my-fucking-parking-spot-again-you-son-of-a-bitch-that's-my-fucking-parking-spot-don't-you-*ever*-fucking-park-there-again-you-cocksucker . . ."

What's the best way to part a girl's hair?
With your tongue.

Jackie "The Joke Man" Martling's

Paul works in the circus, following the elephants with a pail and shovel. One day, his brother comes to see him.

He says, "Paul, I've got great news. I've got you a job in my office. You'll wear a suit and tie, work regular hours, and start at thirteen five. How about it?"

Paul says, "*What?* And give up *show business?*"

I'm glad you're enjoying my book.
Jeeze, I haven't seen a smile like that since Captain Hook wiped with the wrong hand.

How are a woman's breasts like
electric train sets?
*They were originally intended for
the kids, but Pop always winds
up playing with them.*

Mehrtens is a traveling salesman, and his car breaks down, so he has to spend the night at a farmer's house. There's only one place for him to sleep, and that's in the bed with the farmer and his beautiful daughter. The three of them climb into bed, and the farmer finally falls asleep.

Mehrtens whispers to the girl, "Let's get it on."

She says, "You better see if my father's asleep."

Mehrtens unbuttons the flap of the farmer's pajamas, reaches in, and yanks a hair out of the farmer's rear end. The farmer doesn't stir, so they get it on.

A little while later, Mehrtens says to the girl, "Hey, let's do it again."

She says, "Make sure my father is asleep."

Mehrtens reaches in and pulls another hair out of his butt. The farmer doesn't budge, so they do it again.

It's almost sunrise, and Mehrtens says, "What do you say? One more time?"

She says, "Make sure my father is asleep."

Mehrtens reaches in and grabs another hair, and *yanks!* it, but it doesn't come out. He gives it another good tug, but the hair just doesn't come out.

All of a sudden the farmer wakes up, rolls over, and says, "Listen, Mac, I don't care if you fuck my daughter, but don't keep score on my ass."

How is a pussy like a grapefruit?
The best ones squirt when you eat them.

Why don't the cheerleaders in San Francisco
wear short skirts?
*Because when they sit down
their balls hang out.*

Hodgee comes to the United States from India, and he's only here a few months when he gets very ill. He goes to doctor after doctor, but none of them can help him. Finally, he goes to an Indian doctor.

The doctor says, "Take dis bucket, go into de other room, shit in de bucket, piss on de shit, and then put your head down over de bucket and breathe in de fumes for ten minutes."

Hodgee takes the bucket, goes into the other room, shits in the bucket, pisses on the shit, bends over, and breathes in the fumes for ten minutes.

Then he comes back to the doctor and says, "It worked. I feel *terrific.* What was it?"

The doctor says, "You were homesick."

Chiusano says to his wife, "How about a quickie?"
She says, "As opposed to *what?*"

A construction worker goes to the doctor and says, "Doc, I'm constipated."

The doctor examines him for a minute and then says, "Lean over the table."

The construction worker leans over the table, the doctor *whacks!* him on the ass with a baseball bat, and then sends him into the bathroom.

He comes out a few minutes later and says, "Doc, I feel great. What should I do?"

The doctor says, "Stop wiping with cement bags."

There once was a guy from Sydney,
Who could put it in up to her kidney,
But a guy from Quebec,
Put it up to her neck,
He had a big one, didn't he?

What would you call a German tampon?
A twatstika.

Zebrowski gets home from work early, walks in the front door, and there's a guy on the living room floor banging his wife.

He says, "Sylvia, what are you *doing?*"

She says, "I *told* you he was stupid."

Why do Jewish guys watch porno movies backwards?
*Because they like the part where the hooker
gives the money back.*

How was Velcro invented?
*An Italian woman was trying to pull on a wool sweater over
her head, and it got caught on her mustache.*

Why don't witches wear any underwear?
So they can get a better grip on their broomsticks.

Reeb marries a girl, and they go on their honeymoon. He leaves the room the first night to go down to the lobby to get a pack of cigarettes, and when he gets back, his bride is lying on the bed naked fucking one of the bellhops. Another one is under her, getting her in the ass, she's sucking off the desk clerk, and she's jerking off a cab driver and the dishwasher.

Reeb screams, "What the fuck are all these jag-offs doing in here?"

She says, "Well, you always knew I was a flirt."

Why don't women blink during foreplay?
They don't have time.

What's the difference between a band leader
and a gynecologist?
A band leader fucks *his* singers.

I hope you enjoyed this section.
*If you didn't, why don't you go
run through a harp.*

Nipple Hair

Elkins is out hunting and he sees a bear. He shoots, and the bear falls. He goes running up, and there's no bear. There's a tap on his shoulder, he turns around, and it's the bear.

The bear says, "Did you just shoot at me?"

Elkins says, "Yeah."

The bear points at his dick and says, "Suck my cock."

What can he do, it's a bear. So he sucks the bear's cock. He swallows. (That has nothing to do with the joke, but I like to promote that wherever I can.)

Elkins goes to the gun shop and buys a double-barrel shotgun. He goes into the woods, sees the bear, fires both barrels, and the bear falls. He goes running up, and there's no bear. There's a tap on his shoulder, and it's the bear.

The bear says, "Did you just shoot at me twice with a double-barrel shotgun?"

Elkins says, "Yeah."

The bear says, "Pull down your pants and bend over that log."

What can he do, it's a bear. He pulls down his pants, bends over the log, and the bear fucks him in the ass. And it takes a long time, because the bear just had sex the day before.

The next day Elkins goes to the gun shop and buys an elephant gun. He goes into the forest, spots the bear, empties the gun into it, and the bear falls. He goes running up, and there's no bear. There's a tap on his shoulder.

He turns around and the bear says, "You don't come here to *hunt,* do you?"

Jackie "The Joke Man" Martling's

Phelan turns on his TV in a San Francisco motel room and sees a local ad with two guys in it.

The first guy says, "Is this margarine?"

The second guy says, "Yes, it's margarine."

The first guy says, "Well, it *feels* like *butter.*"

What's the difference between spit and swallow?

Forty pounds of pressure on the back of her head.

Hiram answers the telephone, and it's an emergency room doctor.

The doctor says, "Your wife was in a serious car accident, and I have bad news and good news. The bad news is she has lost all use of both arms and both legs, and will be on a respirator the rest of her life."

Hiram says, "My God. What's the good news?"

The doctor says, "I'm kidding. She's dead."

Colleen is a devout Catholic, a very religious girl. She gets married, and has seventeen children, and then her husband dies.

She doesn't get married again for two weeks. Then she has twenty-two children by her next husband, and then *he* dies. A few months later, Colleen dies.

At the funeral, the priest looks skyward and says, "At last, they're together."

A guy sitting in the front says, "Excuse me, Father, but do you mean her and her *first* husband, or her and her *second* husband?"

The priest says, "I mean her *legs.*"

Here we are in the classroom, and the teacher draws a huge penis on the blackboard.

She says, "Can anyone tell me what this is?"

Dirty Johnny stands up and says, "Yup. I know what it is. It's a penis. And you know how I know? My old man's got *two* of 'em."

The teacher says, "*Two* of them? Are you sure, son?"

Johnny says, "Of course I'm sure. The little one he uses to pee, and the big one he uses to brush the babysitter's teeth."

A guy from France, a guy from California, and a guy from New York get caught by cannibals.

They say to the guy from France, "We're going to boil you and eat you."

He says, "Sacre bleu! Zis is terrible! You cannot boil me and eat me! Sacre bleu!"

They say to the guy from California, "We're going to cut you up, and use your bones to make weapons."

The guy from California says, "Oh, wow, man, you can't do that, man . . . you can't cut me up and use my bones, man . . . that's bogus, dudes."

They say to the New Yorker, "And *you*. We're going to peel off all of your skin, and use it to make a canoe."

The New Yorker grabs a fork from one of the cannibals, starts stabbing himself all over, and he says, "Yeah? Here's your fucking canoe, you asshole. I got your fucking canoe right here. Here's your fucking canoe, Jack. Your mother should take a trip in *this* canoe, you fucking cocksucker."

Why should you fuck a mountain goat
on the edge of a cliff?
So you'll be sure she pushes back.

A dentist says to his patient, "You just had oral sex with your wife, didn't you?"

The guy says, "Why do you say that, Doc? Does my breath smell?"

The dentist says, "No."

The guy says, "Pubic hair in my teeth?"

The dentist says, "No."

The guy says, "So how'd you know?"

The dentist says, "You've got shit on your nose."

How is a woman like a toilet seat?
*Without the hole in the middle, they
wouldn't be good for shit.*

A Polish guy takes a girl to the drive-in.
She says, "Do you want to get in the back seat?"
He says, "Oh, no. I'm staying up here with *you*."

Perkins tells a stranger at the bar that he's about to get married to Betsy, the waitress in the restaurant on the corner.

The stranger says, "*Betsy?* Shit, I've known that bimbo for ten years. Brown hair, but her pussy hair is a lot darker?"

Perkins says, "That's right."

"Has an ostrich tattooed on her lower belly with its head buried in her snatch?"

"That's the one."

"Loves every kind of kinky sex, and can't ever seem to get it up her asshole enough?"

"Yep."

"I must have banged her five hundred goddamned times."

Perkins calls the bartender over and says, "Sir, please give this man a drink on me. He's a friend of my fiancée."

How do you ditch a Jewish cop?
Drive through a toll booth.

What's the difference between driving
and getting a blow job?
You can only hold one beer while you're driving.

Brad and Doreen are taking a horse-drawn cab ride in the midst of their fun-packed New York City honeymoon. The carriage goes down a cobblestone avenue, and it causes Doreen to cut an incredibly loud fart. I mean, it isn't often the horse stops and turns around. Being terribly embarrassed, Doreen decides she better start up some kind of conversation.

She says, "Brad, honey, should we stop along the way and pick up a paper?"

Brad says, "Nah. When we go through the park, I'll reach out and grab you a handful of leaves."

Why don't Mexicans wear short-sleeved shirts?
*Because it would be disgusting to
wipe snot on their bare wrists.*

Jackie "The Joke Man" Martling's

"Aaallpp!"

There's a scream from the bedroom. The husband runs in and there's a guy leaping out of the window.

His wife says, *"Whaa!* That guy just fucked me twice!"

He says, *"Twice?* Why didn't you call me in after he fucked you *once?"*

She says, "Because I thought it was you . . . until he started for the second one."

Why did the Italians lose the war?
They ordered ziti instead of shells.

Salem says to his wife, "If I said something was *black,* you'd say it was *white,* just to disagree, wouldn't you?"

She says, "No."

Dirty Johnny gets a newspaper route. He rings a bell and a lady answers wearing just a bra and panties.

He says, "Collect, miss. That'll be five dollars."

She says, "I'm a little short on cash, but if you want, I'll give you sex instead."

Johnny says, "All right."

He walks in, she unfastens his pants, and pulls them down, and there's the biggest dick she's ever seen. Like a baby's arm with an apple in its fist. Veins the size of pencils, a *monster.* He reaches into his shirt pocket, pulls out a handful of huge washers, and starts sliding them onto his prick.

She says, "What are you doing? I can take it all."

He says, "Not for five bucks you can't."

Did you hear about the Ethiopian who
fell into the alligator pit?
She ate three of them before they
could get her out of there.

I hope you enjoyed this section.
If you didn't, why don't you just close the book and pout like you've got a turd caught sideways?

Douches
Are Wild

A couple has been dating for three months, and the sex is getting dull.

One night they're lying in bed when the girl says, "Harry, want to try something new? It's very kinky."

He says, "Sure."

She says, "Stand over me and take a shit on me."

He stands up, straddles her, squats a bit, and takes a dump on her chest.

She says, "Now lie in it on top of me and fuck me."

He lies on top of her, with the shit oozing between them, and she gives him the wildest fuck he's ever had. The next time they're lying in bed, it's boring, and she asks him to do it again. He stands over her and grinds out a huge chocolate Carvel onto her chest. Then he lies on her, and they have another incredible fuck. As time goes on, Harry really gets into it. He eats like a horse on the days before their dates, because it seems the more he craps on her, the better the sex is.

One Thursday night, he has the runs, so on Friday morning he eats a few cheese sandwiches and downs a whole bottle of Kaopectate before he goes to work, so he won't wheedle down his legs at the office. That night, he goes to her house, they go into the bedroom and get undressed, she lies on the bed, he stands over her, and squats down, and grunts . . . but nothing comes out. He strains a bit, and grunts, and then *llbbt!* . . . a little fart . . . but nothing of any substance. For a few minutes, he's pushing and grunting, when suddenly he hears her crying.

He says, "Honey, what's wrong?"

She says, "You don't love me anymore."

Jackie "The Joke Man" Martling's

What's the difference between St. Patrick's
Day and Martin Luther King Day?
*On St. Patrick's Day, everybody wishes
they were Irish.*

McCreedy goes up to the drugstore counter and says, "I
need some condoms and some pesticide."

The girl says, "Don't you mean *spermicide?*"

He says, "No, I mean *pesticide.* My wife's got a bug up
her ass and I'm goin' in after it."

Bernstein and Nickau are walking along when a beautiful girl comes walking the other way.

Nickau says, "Let's fuck her."

Bernstein says, "Fuck her out of *what?*"

What's the quietest place in the world?
*The complaint department at the
parachute packing plant.*

What's the worst thing about a lung transplant?
Coughing up someone else's phlegm.

A guy walks into a bar and there's a gorilla sitting in the corner.

He says to the bartender, "What's with the gorilla?"

The bartender says, "I'll show you."

He takes a baseball bat from behind the bar, walks around, and *smashes!* the gorilla in the forehead with the baseball bat. The gorilla drops to his knees, and gives the bartender a blow job.

When the gorilla gets done, the bartender says, "What do you think?"

The guy says, "That's great."

The bartender says, "You want to try?"

The guy says, "Okay. But don't hit me so hard."

Baer is whittling, he doesn't realize his zipper's open, and he almost cuts off his dick.

His dick looks up and says, "You know, we've had a lot of fistfights, but I never thought you'd pull a *knife* on me."

Do black people really talk funny?
No. It's a miff.

Do you know what a "will-not" is?
*A "will-not" is a little tiny ball of toilet paper that gets stuck
in the hairs of your ass and* will not *come out.*

An Eskimo's snowblower is on the blink, so he takes it to get fixed.

The mechanic works on it a while, and then he says to the Eskimo, "Looks like you blew a seal."

The Eskimo says, "No, it's just snot."

"Pop, can I have twenty dollars for a blow job?"
"I don't know, son. Are you any good?"

Roberts is sitting with his wife at a football game. Every few minutes, somebody comes over and fondles her. They squeeze her tits, reach up her dress, finger her, grind against her knees. And Roberts just sits there and accepts it.

Finally, the guy sitting next to him says, "Don't you see what the hell is going on?"

Roberts says, "Of course."

The guy says, "Why'd you bring her to the game?"

Roberts says, "Because if I leave her home, everybody goes to my house and fucks her."

An optometrist operates on a hippie painter's girlfriend and saves her eyesight. The hippie painter is so grateful that he goes to the doctor's house one day while the doctor has office hours, goes inside, and paints a huge eye on an entire wall of the living room, leaving the fireplace as the pupil of the eye. He's just finishing up when the doctor walks in.

He says to the doctor, "Well, do you like it, man?"

The doctor says, "Yeah, but I'll tell you, I'm certainly glad I'm not a gynecologist."

Why do Arab women wear veils?
*So they can blow their noses without
getting their hands dirty.*

Two bananas are laying on a river bank when a turd comes floating by.

The turd looks over at the two bananas and says, "Come on in! The water's great!"

One banana turns to the other and says, "Do you believe that shit?"

What does a seventy-year-old snatch taste like?
Depends.

West says to the doctor, "Doc, my hearing's going. I can't even hear myself fart."

The doctor says, "Take these pills every day for a week."

West says, "Will they make me hear better?"

The doctor says, "They'll make you fart louder."

Mrs. Blum's husband has lost all interest in sex, so she goes and buys some crotchless panties. That night she takes off all of her clothes, puts on the crotchless panties, and lies on the bed.

When her husband walks in from work, she yells, "I'm in here."

When he walks in, she spreads her legs and says, "You see anything you want?"

He says, "Why would I want any of *that?* Look what it did to your panties."

A couple's been married for fifteen years, and they sleep in separate beds. One night the husband is really horny. He's got a marble hard-on, a boner a cat couldn't scratch.

He says, "Hon-ey! Why don't you come over to daddy-poo and daddy make whoopee with mommy? Daddy loves mommy."

She says, "All right."

She gets out of her bed, and on her way over she trips over the rug in the middle.

The guy says, "Oh, poopsie, are you all right? Did my little babycakes hurt her toesie-woesies? Come to me, honeybunch."

She gets in and he fucks her hard. They get done, she gets out of his bed, and on the way back she trips over the rug again.

He says, "You clumsy *bitch.*"

Mrs. Simpson is on her deathbed, and she says to her husband, "Will you ride with my mother on the way to the grave?"

He says, "All right, but it's going to ruin my whole day."

A little girl walks out of the bathroom, and her mother's making a cake.

She says, "Mommy, can I lick the bowl?"

Her mother says, "Will you *flush* it like everyone else?"

It's medieval times, and the coach of the queen of England and the coach of the queen of Spain approach each other on a narrow dirt road. It's an impasse, and neither is prepared to yield the right of way.

The coach driver for the queen of England stands up proudly, and says, "Make way for the Lord Majesty, her Nobleness, the Queen of England, the ruler to the north, to the south, to the east, to the west, the ruler of the serfs, the peasants, the land barons and the servants, the ruler of the greatest kingdom in this or any other world. Make way for the queen of England. Make way for the *queen*."

The coach driver for the queen of Spain stands up and says, "Hey, yo, what'ya think I got in *here? A* bag of *shit?*"

Cronin goes to see a psychiatrist.

He says, "Doc, I can't seem to make friends. Can you help me, you fat slob?"

Two guys are walking down the street. The guy on the left is dragging his right leg, and the guy on the right is dragging his left leg.

The guy on the right says to the guy on the left, "What happened to you, man?"

He says, "Vietnam, 1969. What about you?"

He says, "Dog shit, about two blocks back."

Two gay guys are taking a shower when the phone rings.

The first guy says, "I'll get it, but don't come, *don't come.*"

He answers the phone, and when he comes back there's sperm everywhere.

He says, "I told you not to come."

The other guy says, "I *didn't* come. I farted."

I hope you enjoyed this section.
If you didn't, I have a feeling you came from a wad your mom should have swallowed.

My Turn
in the Barrel

A group of English gentlemen are sitting around in the den of a London men's club, and it's a special gathering, because the oldest member, Colonel Rowlinson, is there.

One of the men says, "Colonel, why don't you tell us a tale from one of your exploits?"

Colonel Rowlinson says, "Well, there was a time years ago when we were trekking through the Kenyan jungle. The fuzzy-tops were quite tired, what with carrying all the bundles as they cleared a path through the dense underbrush. We came to a clearing, so we sat to have a spot of tea and regain our strength, when suddenly, out of the foliage, leaps a nine-foot tiger. *Rrrooaarrr!* My God, I shit myself."

One of the gentlemen says, "Well, Colonel, that's perfectly under*standable*, what with a huge *tiger* coming at you."

The Colonel says, "Not *then*, you blithering idiot. Just *now*, when I went, *'Rrrooaarr.'*"

What would you call 3.1416 vaginas?
Hair pi.

Schick is walking down the boardwalk in Atlantic City, runs into a hooker, and he says, "How much?"

She says "Twenty bucks."

He says, "All right."

They climb down under the boardwalk, and he bangs her. The next night, he runs into the same hooker, they go under the boardwalk, only this time while he's banging her, she blasts two incredible farts. When they get done, he hands her twenty-*five* dollars.

She says, "What's the extra five?"

He says, "That's for blowing the sand off my balls."

What animal has an asshole in the middle of its back?
Prince Charles's horse.

A big, fat farmer is walking down a dirt road in the rain with his big, fat wife when he suddenly gets horny. He pulls her down to the ground, lifts up her dress, and starts fucking her. After a minute, he says, "Elsie, is it in you, or is it in the mud?"

She says, "It's in the mud."

He reaches down and fiddles around a bit, and then he says, "Now is it in you, or is it in the mud?"

She says, "It's in me."

He says, "Put it back in the mud."

A blind guy goes into a whorehouse. A girl takes him upstairs and starts giving him a blow job.

He says to her, "Excuse me, aren't you Karen Snyder, and didn't you go to Lincoln Park High in Detroit?"

She says, "Yes. How'd you know?"

He says, "I never forget a face."

What would you call a lesbian with thick fingers?
Well-hung.

Marcela's mother is constantly riding her about getting married.

Every day, her mother says, "You're thirty-two, and you've never been married. You're thirty-two, and you've never even been engaged. Never married, never engaged. You've gotta get married."

She says, "Leave me alone, Ma, leave me alone."

Her mother goes on and on, "You've gotta get married. You've gotta get married. You've gotta get married."

She says, "Ma, leave me a*lone.*"

One day she walks into the house, and she's got rice in her hair.

Her mother says, "You did it! You finally got married!"

She says, "No. I was blowing a chink and he threw up on my head."

What is the definition of making love?
*That's what a woman is doing while
a guy is fucking her.*

Tarzan gets in a terrible fight with a ferocious lion, and loses an eye, an arm, and his dick. The animals of the jungle nurse Tarzan back to health. They give him the eye of a hawk, the arm of a gorilla, and for a pecker, they give him a baby elephant's trunk.

After about a week, Cheetah comes up to Tarzan and says, "How Tarzan like new parts?"

Tarzan says, "Eye good. Tarzan see far, clear. Arm good. Long, strong. But Tarzan not crazy about new weenie. All day long, pick weeds, stuff up Tarzan's ass."

What's the difference between a
white cow and a black cow?
*A white cow goes, "Moo," and a black
cow goes, "Moo out de way."*

A mother and her daughter are walking along the beach. The girl says, "Mom, do you think I'm old enough to start douching?"

Her mother says, "Why don't you ask all the seagulls behind you?"

Why don't black people become astronauts?
Because they don't like to say
"Yes, NASA", "No, NASA."

A lady walks into her daughter's room, and her daughter's doing herself with her vibrator.

She says, "My God! What are you doing?"

Her daughter says, "Ma, I'm forty years old. I don't even have a boyfriend. I'll never get married, so *this* is my husband."

A few minutes later, her father walks in, and she's doing herself with the vibrator.

He says "My God! What are you doing?"

She says "Daddy, I'm forty years old. I don't even have a boyfriend. I'll never get married, so *this* is my husband."

The next day, the mother and daughter go out shopping. When they get home, they walk into the kitchen, and there's the father. He's got a martini in one hand and he's got the vibrator buzzing away in his ass.

Her mother says, "My God! What are *you* doing?"

He says, "I'm having a drink with my new son-in-law."

A guy walks into a delicatessen and says, "Could I have a baloney?"

The counterman says, "You want me to slice it up?"

The guy says, "Does my fanny look like a piggy bank?"

The wife says, "Chris, you're *a sex maniac.*"

He says, "Get out of this bed, and take your fucking sisters with you."

Rosegarten goes to the doctor, and after the examination, the doctor says, "Well, my friend, you've got VD."

Rosegarten says, "Well, Doc, I must have caught it from a toilet seat."

The doctor says, "Well, then you must have been chewing on it. You've got it in your gums."

A duck walks into a 7-11, waddles up to the counter, and says, "Have you got any grapes?"

The guy behind the counter says, "No," and the duck leaves.

The next day the duck walks into the 7-11 and says, "Have you got any grapes?"

The guy says, "No!", and the duck leaves.

The next day the duck walks into the 7-11 and says, "Have you got any grapes?"

The guy says, "Listen, Daffy, this is the third day in a row I'm telling you, we haven't got any grapes. If you walk in here and ask me again, I'm gonna nail your stupid webbed feet to the floor."

The next day the duck walks into the 7-11 and says, "Do you have any nails?"

The guy says, "No."

The duck says, "Good. Have you got any grapes?"

What's the best thing about a blow job?
Ten minutes of peace and quiet.

What's the definition of a nice Greek boy?
*A Greek boy who takes a girl out twice
before he fucks her brother.*

What should you do if a woman tells you she
faked her orgasm?
Pretend you didn't hear her.

What does it mean when the flag at the
Post Office is flying at half mast?
They're hiring.

What's the difference between a rabbi and a priest?
A rabbi cuts it off, and a priest sucks it off.

*Did you know at the amusement park in
San Francisco before you go into the tunnel
of love you have to dress up as a gerbil?*

The firemen finally get a huge fire under control, and Chief Mattea has all of his men accounted for except Olson and Rosolino. After a few minutes' search, the chief looks down an alley, and there's Rosolino, leaning over a trash can. His pants are down to his ankles, and Olson is fucking him in the ass.

Chief Mattea says, "What the hell is going on?"

Olson says, "Rosolino passed out from smoke inhalation."

The chief says, "Smoke inhalation? You're supposed to give him mouth-to-mouth resuscitation."

Olson says, "I did, Chief. That's how this shit got started."

What's the difference between a
homo and a hunting dog?
A hunting dog sics ducks.

Stellar walks into a bar and has seven beers. Then he looks around until he finds the prettiest girl in the bar. He walks up to her and says, "Do you want to fuck?"

She screams, "You *pig*," *smashes!* him over the head with her purse, and knocks him across the bar with a bar stool.

He picks himself up, walks to the bar, and has seven more beers. Then he walks up to her again, and says, "I guess a blow job is out of the question?"

I hope you enjoyed this section.
*If you didn't, why don't you go
suck on a horse's ass until its
head caves in?*

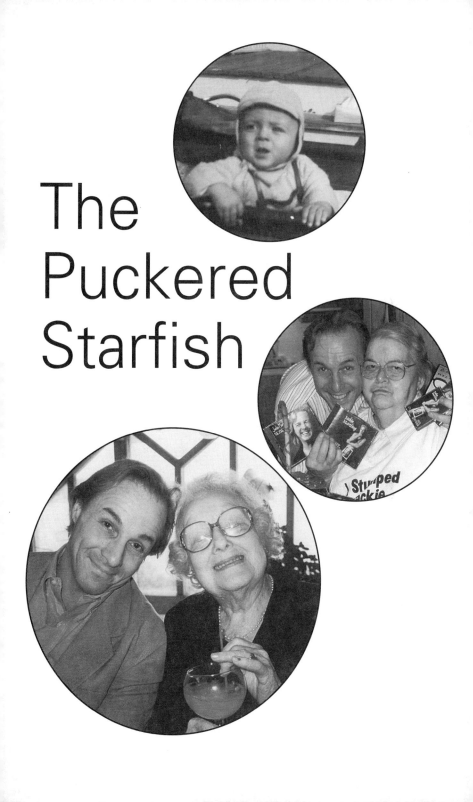

The Puckered Starfish

What was Helen Keller's worst day?
*When she burned her mouth on a slice of pizza
and couldn't taste anything, either.*

Haberman comes before the judge.

The judge says, "Why are you here?"

Haberman says, "I beat my wife to death with a golf club."

The judge says, "How many strokes did it take you?"

Did you hear about the guy who had a
wet dream and fell asleep before he was through?

Did you hear about Adolph, the
brown-nosed reindeer?
*He could run as fast as Rudolph,
he just couldn't stop as fast.*

How do you say constipated in German?
"Farfrumpoopen."

Einziger says to Reiber, "What part of a girl is her *yet?*"
Reiber says, "I don't know. Why?"
Einziger says, "It says in the paper that a girl was shot in Brooklyn yesterday and they haven't been able to get the bullet out of her yet."

Frawley and Fotré are in a bar arguing about who's got the biggest dick. The bartender says, "Look, there's nobody else in here. Take 'em out and put 'em on the bar, and we'll see once and for all who's got the biggest dick."

They agree, and they're just taking them out and putting them on the bar when another guy walks in.

The bartender says, "Can I get you a drink?"

The guy says, "No, I'll just help myself to the buffet."

What's sixty-eight?
Blow me and I'll owe you one.

A hillbilly kid walks into a Nashville whorehouse and says, "I want a woman, but I've always been scared, because my momma told me a woman has teeth between her legs."

The whore says, "Don't be silly. I'll take care of you."

She brings him up to a room, gets undressed, lies on the bed, spreads her legs, and says, "See? No teeth."

The kid says, "How the hell could you have teeth down there? Look at the shape your gums are in."

Why don't Arabs circumcise their camels?
So they have a place to put their gum in a sandstorm.

Did you hear about the Polish gangster?
His career is managed by three black singers.

What do fat women do in the summer?
Stink.

Borders picks up a hitchhiker, and before he takes off, the hitchhiker pulls out a gun and tells him to jerk off. So he does. Then the hitchhiker tells him to do it again. So he does it again. No sooner does he finish the second time, the hitch-hiker tells him to do it one more time. After pumping and pumping and pumping, he finally finishes the third time. Then the hitchhiker gets out of the car and a pretty girl gets in.

The hitchhiker says to Borders, "Now will you do me a favor and give my sister a ride to the next town?"

Why are Jewish children so obnoxious?
Heredity.

One night, Pinocchio's girlfriend says to him, "This stinks. Every time we make love I get splinters."

So Pinocchio goes to Gepetto to ask his advice.

Gepetto says, "Sandpaper, my boy, that's all you need."

A few days later Gepetto runs into Pinocchio and says, "So how are you doing with the girls now?"

Pinocchio says, "Who needs girls?"

Bleiweiss dies, and goes to hell.

The devil tells him, "You have your pick of three different rooms. Follow me."

They go to the first room, the devil opens the door, and everyone is treading water in piss. They go to the second room, the devil opens the door, and everyone is up to their necks in shit. They go to the third room, the devil opens the door, and everyone is sitting in chairs, drinking coffee, with diarrhea pooled up to their knees.

Bleiweiss says to the devil, "I'll definitely take the third room."

He goes into the third room, gets a cup of coffee, and before he gets a chance to sit down, the devil yells, "All right, on your heads, coffee break's over."

Why do Sumo wrestlers shave their legs?
So nobody will mistake them for lesbians.

What goes peck, peck, *bang!?*
A chicken in a minefield.

Newman walks into a whorehouse and says to the madam, "I want something really raunchy. That's the kind of mood I'm in."

The madam smiles and says, "I have just the girl for you. Rebel Rosie. She's had every dick in Dixie. She can suck the chrome off a trailer hitch. Go up to the first room on the right, and I'll send her up right away."

Newman says, "Thanks. Oh, and could you have her bring a couple of bottles of beer, too?"

The madam says, "Sure."

Newman goes up to the room and waits. A few minutes later, in walks Rosie, and is she a beast. Her face could knock a bulldog off a meat wagon. She puts the beers on the dresser, takes off all her clothes, and gets down on the floor on all fours.

Newman says, "No, no, Rosie, get in the bed, I just want to do it regular style."

Rosie says, "Okay. I just thought you might want to open the beers first."

Why was the cheerleader black and blue from gonorrhea?
Because she gave it to one of the football players.

What do you find in a clean nose?
Fingerprints.

Did you hear about "The Divorce Barbie"?
It comes with all of Ken's shit.

A lady says to her husband, "Howard, I want breast implants."

He says, "We can't afford it. Go grab a wad of toilet paper and rub it up and down between your tits."

She says, "Will it make them bigger?"

He says, "It worked on your ass."

I hope you enjoyed this section.
If you didn't, why don't you go shit and fall back in it?

A Feather in
My Crap

Charlie picks up a woman in a bar. They get in his car, and they're going down a dirt road to lover's lane, when he gets a flat tire. He looks in the trunk, and his spare is flat, too. He figures, what the hell, he's gonna get a little bit. So they get in the back seat, and he's just getting off her blouse and her bra, when another car pulls up.

He gets out, and the other guy says, "Can I help you?"

Charlie says, "You sure can. I'll tell you what . . . if you'll let me use your car to go get my spare fixed, you can pork the babe in the back seat while I'm gone."

The guy says, "You're on."

The guy gives him the keys, Charlie puts his spare tire in the guy's trunk, and takes off. The guy gets in the back seat, hops on the girl, and they're just about to go to it when a police car pulls up.

A cop walks over, shines the flashlight into the back seat, and says, "What are you doing, Mac?"

The guy says, "I'm just about to bang my wife, officer."

The cop says, "I'm sorry, pal, I didn't realize it was your wife."

The guy says, "Neither did I, 'til you shined your flashlight on her."

What happens if a girl doesn't
wear undies in the winter?
She gets chapped lips.

A snotty rich lady goes in to see a doctor and she says, "Doctor, I am very wealthy, and I have always had anything I've wanted. But I've never, ever experienced what it's like to be pregnant. I would like you to perform some kind of procedure on me, so I may see what it's like to be pregnant."

He says, "All right, lady."

He takes her into the examination room, works on her a while, and then she leaves.

A couple of hours later she calls up, and she says, "Doctor, it has been *hours,* and I do not yet feel pregnant."

He says, "You will in a few days, lady. I stitched your ass shut."

Schirripa is drowning. The lifeguard swims out, drags him in, puts him on the edge of the shore, and starts pumping his arms. Water starts spurting out of Schirripa's mouth. The lifeguard keeps pumping his arms, and out comes fish . . . and clams . . . and seaweed . . .

Gange comes walking along and says, "Hey, you better get his asshole out of the water, you're gonna empty the ocean."

Rydzewski meets a girl in a bar, they get in his car, and she sucks his cock for hours. About two o'clock in the morning, he pulls into the driveway, reaches in his glove compartment, takes out a resin bag, and rubs it on his hands. He walks in the house, and his wife's standing there waiting for him.

She says, "Where have you been?"

He says, "I was out getting my dick sucked all night."

She grabs his hands and looks at them and says, "Look at the resin on your hands, you lying son-of-a-bitch. You were *bowling*."

What's the difference between a drunk
and an alcoholic?
*A drunk doesn't have to go to those
stupid meetings.*

Oprah goes to the doctor with a sore throat, and he says, "Take off all of your clothes, lie on your back on my table, and spread your legs as wide as you can."

She says, "How will that help my sore throat?"

He says, "It won't, but I want to see how my house will look painted black with pink shutters."

Hennessey is the town drunk, but they feel sorry for him, so they give him a job at the morgue checking on the bodies. One night he starts on the Jack Daniels early. As he's going along, checking the bodies, he pulls out a tray, the body is upside-down, and its sphincter starts wailing, "My wild Irish rose . . ."

He can't believe it. He pushes the drawer in, pulls it out again, and it starts again, "My wild Irish rose . . ."

He shuts the drawer, and calls his boss, the coroner.

He slobbers, "Boss, you've got to be coming over, it's to be something you won't be able to believe."

The coroner, very annoyed, comes down to the morgue. Hennessey leads him to the drawer, pulls it out, and sure enough, the sphincter starts, "My wild Irish rose . . ."

The coroner turns to Hennessey and says, "Do you mean to tell me that you got me out of bed at four o'clock in the morning just to hear some asshole sing 'My Wild Irish Rose'?"

Why did the Mexican put ice cubes up his nose?
To keep his lunch cold.

Why do women fake orgasms?
Because they think we care.

A lady catches her kid jerking off.

She says, "Son, don't do that. Save it 'til you're twenty-one."

By the time he was twenty-one, he had nine jars.

Why did the gay guy stop having anal sex
with his lifemate?
Every night it was the same shit.

Dixon and Woods are sitting at the bar, and Dixon says, "My marriage sucks. When I walk in that door, I want that house clean, I want my dinner on the table, and when I'm done eating, I want her to suck my dick, and then it's see you later."

Woods says, "Why's she gotta know your schedule?"

What would you call an open can of tuna fish
in a lesbian's apartment?
Potpourri.

Seefranz is getting married on Saturday. Friday night, his friends take him out and get him waylaid, bylaid, rolaid, mislaid, up, down, up, *bing! bang! boom!*, and forget it, his pecker is a mangled mess. He doesn't know what to do. He takes two popsicle sticks, puts them alongside his dick, and wraps it with adhesive tape. The next day he gets married, and here they are in their honeymoon suite.

She walks out stark naked, and says, "Look, honey. Untouched by human hands."

He's gotta think quick . . . he pulls down his pants and says, "Look! *Hah!* Not even out of the *crate.*"

An Irish girl comes home from college, and she says, "Mother, I've got me a case of VD."

Her mother says, "Put it in the cellar, your old man'll drink anything."

What's the white stuff you find in the
bottom of girls' undies?
Clitty litter.

What would you call a Polish guy who works at
the Post Office?
Overqualified.

A businessman is going on a long trip and he has to take his secretary, who's really got the hots for him. The first night on the train, she's in the top bunk and he's in the bottom bunk.

She says, "Mr. Sirota! Mr. Sirota! I'm cold! I think I need a *blan*ket!"

He says, "Miss Tobin, how'd you like to pretend you're *Mrs.* Sirota for a little while?"

She says, "Oh, I'd *like* that."

He says, "Then get your *own* fucking blanket."

Polish car pool?
They meet at work.

Mullin is talking to Martling when an ambulance goes by and drowns out their conversation.

After it's passed, Mullin says, "Martling, I *hate* that sound. I *hate* the sound of an ambulance. My first wife ran away with an ambulance driver, and every time I hear a siren, I get the shakes thinking he might be bringing her back."

An Englishman comes home early from work and finds his wife on the living room floor with two strange guys. She's blowing one guy and the other guy is fucking her from behind.

The husband says, "'Ello, 'ello."

She says, "So you're not speakin' to *me*, then?"

Two midgets go into an Alaskan convent.

The first midget goes up to the Mother Superior and says, "Hey, lady, you got any midget nuns here?"

She says, "Midget nuns? No."

He says to the other midget, "I told you you fucked a penguin."

How can you tell if a girl's been on a wild date?
She tosses her panties and they stick to the ceiling.

Why do Jewish guys die before their wives?
They want to.

Why can't Avon ladies walk fast?
Their lipstick.

I hope you enjoyed this section. *If you didn't, please remember I perform at weddings, if your parents ever want to get married.*

Name
That Tuna

A couple is driving down the highway when a cop pulls them over.

The cop walks up and says, "You were doing eighty-five in a fifty-five."

The guy says, "You know, officer, I was doing sixty the whole time, and then the last few minutes, I guess I was just keeping up with traffic and I wasn't watching . . ."

His wife says, "That's not true. You were doing eighty-five or ninety the whole time."

He turns to her and says, "Shut the fuck up."

The cop says, "And I notice you haven't got your seat belt buckled."

He says, "Well, officer, I did have it buckled, but then I had to undo it to get my wallet out to show you my license."

His wife says, "That's not true. You haven't had it on the whole time."

He turns to her and says, "What the fuck is wrong with you? Shut up!"

The cop walks around to the wife's side, motions for her to roll down the window, and he says, "Does he always talk to you like that?"

She says, "Only when he's drunk."

What's seventy-one?
When you're sixty-nine'ing and you stick a
finger in each other's asshole.

Here we are, out in the country, and Maw walks in and says, "Jethro, get out there and fix that there outhouse."

He says, "All right, Maw."

He walks out to the outhouse, looks at it, and says, "Maw, there ain't nothin' *wrong* with this here *outhouse.*"

She says, "Put your head down in the hole."

He puts his head down in the hole and he says, "Maw, there ain't nothin' *wrong* with this here *outhouse.*"

He goes to lift up his head and he says, "Oww! *Oww!* Maw! *Maw,* my *beard's* stuck!"

She says, "It's aggravatin', ain't it?"

A Jewish girl comes home and says, "Ma, I got married."

Her mother says, "Oy, that's *great.*"

She says, "But, Ma, he's an Arab."

Her mother says, "Oy, that's *not* so great."

She says, "But, Ma, he's an Arab *sheik.* He's wealthy beyond your *wildest dreams.* You and Daddy are going to live in the lap of luxury for the *rest of your lives.*"

Six months later, she walks in the house and says, "Ma, I love my Arab sheik, but my God, all he wants to do is boff me in my ass. Day and night, that's all he'll do is bang me in my ass. When I got married, my asshole was the size of a dime . . . now, it's the size of a silver dollar."

Her mother says, "So for *ninety cents* you're going to make *trouble?*"

Why should you never drink diet soda
during oral sex?
*Because then you'll have two aftertastes
to get rid of.*

Bloch and DeVino are sitting at a bar when Bloch pulls down his zipper and starts pissing into a beer bottle.

DeVino says, "What are you doing?"

Bloch says, "This shit's so good I'm gonna drink it again."

Freismuth stumbles into a bar.

The bartender says, "Get the hell out of here. You're too drunk to be in here."

Freismuth says, "If I'm so drunk, how come I can see that one-eyed cat walkin' in here?"

The bartender says, "That cat's *leaving*."

Tinker calls home and says, "Honey, I won the lottery. Start packing."

She says, "Should I pack for the beach or to go skiing?"

He says, "I don't care where you go. Just get the fuck *out.*"

Jeni moves into a new neighborhood. The first day in his new house, he walks out on the sidewalk, and he sees the couple across the street through their picture window. The lady has the lawn mower in the living room, and she's mowing the carpet. Her husband has his hand in the goldfish bowl and he's giving her the finger. Jeni runs next door to the Mulrooneys', and he's freaking out as he describes the scene to his new neighbor.

Mulrooney says, "Oh, that's no big deal. They're deaf mutes. She's telling him, 'You better mow the lawn on Saturday,' and he's saying, 'Fuck you, I'm going fishing'."

Giuseppi walks into work, and he says, "Ey, Tony! You know who's-a George Washington?"

Tony says, "No, Giuseppi, who's-a George Washington?"

He says, "Hah! George-a Washington's the first-a President of-a United States. I'm-a go to night school, learn all about-a United States, and become-a U.S.-a citizen."

A couple of days later, Giuseppi walks into work and says, "Ey, Tony, you know who's-a Abraham Lincoln?"

Tony says, "No, Giuseppi, who's-a Abraham Lincoln?"

He says, "Hah! Abraham-a Lincoln is-a sixteenth President of-a the United States. I'm-a go to night school, learn all about-a United States, and become-a U.S.-a citizen."

A guy in the back of the shop yells, "Yo, Giuseppi . . . you know who Fishlips Lorenzo is?"

He says, "No. Who's-a Fishlips Lorenzo?"

The guy yells, "That's the guy who's bangin' your wife while you're in night school."

How do you get a nun pregnant?
Dress her up as an altar boy.

There was an old woman that lived in a shoe,
She had so many children her cunt fell off.

The Polish cowboy, Gene Autrowski, is in the saloon getting drunk, so his friends decide to play a trick on him. They turn his horse around, and then they turn his saddle around, so he won't know.

The next morning, his wife kicks him, and says, "Time to get up, Autrowski. Time to get up and get out on the trail."

He says, "I can't get up. I'm beat, I'm whipped, I'm bushed."

She says, "Get up, you lazy bum. You've been drunk for six weeks. Get up and get out on the trail."

He says, "I can't get up. I'm beat, I'm whipped, I'm bushed. Last night was different. Some son-of-a-bitch cut my horse's head off. I had to lead him home with my finger in his windpipe."

Caramico is really drunk and he hails a taxi.

He says to the driver, "Hey, cabbie, have you got room in the front seat for a case of beer and a few burgers?"

The cabbie says, "Sure."

He goes, *"Bllchh!"*

When does a married guy know he's
jerking off too much?
*When he fucks his wife and feels like
he's cheating on himself.*

Why can't the blacks mug the Jews on Yom Kippur?
Dey fast.

Why did the divorced guy keep a picture of his
ex-wife on top of his TV?
To remind him where his VCR went.

How do we know God is a man?
*Because if God was a woman, sperm
would taste like chocolate.*

Why did the feminist cross the road?
To suck my fucking dick.

What two things do you need to know to be a plumber?
Shit doesn't flow uphill, and don't bite your fingernails.

A huge guy marries a tiny girl, and at the wedding, one of his friends says to him, "How the hell do the two of you have sex?"

The big guy says, "I just sit there, naked, on a chair, she sits on top, and I bob her up and down."

His friend says, "You know, that don't sound too bad."

The big guy says, "Well, it's kind of like jerking off, only I got somebody to talk to."

What do a toilet, a clitoris, and an
anniversary have in common?
Men miss them all.

_____

I hope you enjoyed this section.
*If you didn't, go take a flying fuck
at a rolling doughnut.*

Hot
Dogs and
Donuts

The director of the CIA is testing three new agents, ages twenty-five, thirty-five, and forty-five. He puts each of their wives in one of three rooms.

He hands the twenty-five-year-old a revolver and says, "Go into the room and kill your wife."

The twenty-five-year-old says, "I can't do it. I love her too much."

The director hands the gun to the thirty-five-year-old and says, "Go into the room and kill your wife."

The thirty-five-year-old goes into the room, comes out after five minutes, and says, "I can't do it."

The director hands the gun to the forty-five-year-old and says, "Go into the room and kill your wife."

The forty-five-year-old goes into the room. Three shots ring out, and then there's the sound of scuffling and fighting. The director runs into the room and sees the wife dead on the floor.

He says, "What happened?"

The forty-five-year-old says, "Some asshole put blanks in the gun, so I had to choke her to death."

How does a Mexican know when it's time to eat?
His asshole stops burning.

What's a hump?

A hump is a noun meaning the thing on a camel's back, unless the thing is another camel, in which case it becomes a verb.

Hutchinson is on a plane next to a pretty woman and he asks her what she's reading.

She says, "A book on sexual statistics. It says on the average, the American Indian has the longest penis and Polish men have the thickest penis. By the way, I'm Nancy Sirianni. Who are you?"

He says, "Tonto Kowalski."

What would you call a black electrical technician?

Ohm boy.

A girl goes up to a Jewish guy in a bar and says, "I'll do anything you want for two hundred dollars."

He says, "Paint my house."

A young repair man is working on a middle-aged divorcée's refrigerator. He's wearing a sleeveless T-shirt, he's got rippling muscles, and she can't take her eyes off of him. He starts sweating, and it's driving her crazy. She walks up behind him and starts rubbing his neck and his back. She starts grinding against him a little bit, and soon enough she's hugging him. Next thing you know they're making out, their clothes come off, and he starts fucking her up against the wall. When they get done, he backs up and wipes his forehead.

He looks over, and she's still standing there, wiggling and writhing and moaning, going "Ohh! *Unhh!*"

He says, "What's the matter, lady? Ain't you had enough? Ain't I any good?"

She says, "You were fine. Now will you please help me get this doorknob out of my ass?"

Did you hear about the Polish girl who
dropped her gum in the toilet?
She chewed the shit out of it.

A Jewish child molester . . .
"Hey, kid . . . wanna buy some candy?"

Abelson's got a big pimple in the middle of his forehead. A big, huge pimple, and it won't go away. A big pimple, right in the middle of his forehead. He goes to the doctor.

The doctor examines him and says, "My God, my friend, you've got a penis growing out of the middle of your forehead."

Abelson says, "Oh, no, Doc. What can you do?"

The doctor says, "Don't worry. Once it's fully grown, I can remove it completely."

Abelson says, "What do you mean, *fully grown?* Doc, I can't spend years and years staring at that thing, waiting for it to grow."

The doctor says, "Well, you won't have to stare at it for long. Pretty soon, the balls will cover your eyes."

A very naive British sailor is in a bar in London, meets a very wild girl, and she takes him upstairs. She takes off her pants and her panties.

He looks between her legs, and he says, "What's that?"

She says, "It's me lower mouth."

He says, "What do you mean, *your lower mouth?*"

She says, "Just what I said, it's me lower mouth. It's got a mustache . . . it's got lips."

He says, "'as it got a tongue in it?"

She says, "Not always."

Two gay guys live together, and the first guy says, "Let's play hide and seek. I'll hide, and if you find me, I'll blow you."

The second guy says, "What if I can't find you?"

He says, "I'll be behind the piano."

A girl goes to the gynecologist and he examines her.

He says, "You have acute vaginitis."

She says, "Thank you."

A cop stops his patrol car when he sees a couple sitting on the curb. The guy is laying on his stomach with his pants pulled down, and the girl has her finger in his asshole, and she's reaming away with a vengeance.

The cop says, "What the hell is going on?"

The girl says, "This is my date. When I told him I wouldn't spend the night with him, he started pounding down the booze. Now, he's too drunk to drive me home, so I'm trying to sober him up by making him puke."

The cop says, "That's not gonna make him puke."

She says, "Yeah? Wait'll I switch this finger to his mouth."

Why did the Polish girl stop wearing her training bra?
The wheels were irritating her armpits.

Why do black women have such big purses?
To carry their lipstick.

A lady says to her friend, "You know, I think Larry's lost all interest in our lovemaking."

Her friend says, "Do you follow any kind of a ritual?"

She says, "Yeah. Every night I put on this nightgown that's got a low front and a high back. He used to go crazy when he saw me in it."

Her friend says, "Well, why don't you mix it up a little bit? Try putting it on backward tonight. Then it'll have a low back and a high front. Maybe it'll catch his eye."

That night, she goes into the bathroom and puts her nightgown on backward.

Then she walks into the bedroom, spins around, and says, "Honey, do you notice anything different?"

He says, "Yeah. Tonight the skid marks are in the *front* of that fucking nightgown."

Why do girls fart after they pee?
They can't shake it so they blow it dry.

Michael Jackson and the doctor are walking out of the delivery room after his wife gives birth to their son.
Michael says, "How long before we can have sex?"
The doctor says, "At least wait until he's walking."

Why are divorces so expensive?
Because they're worth it.

Why don't Jews wear penny loafers?
Because they'd get stiff necks from looking down to see if the pennies were still there.

You know you're getting old when the only time
you want it twice is before you've had it once.

Meganck goes to a lady dentist and she's pregnant.
He says, "Congratulations."
She says, "Thank you. It's a boy."
He says, "Oh, you had a sonogram to find out the sex of your baby?"
She says, "No, I used the little metal thing with the mirror on the end, and I had a look."

There's nothing quite like going home at two
with a ten and waking up at ten with a two.

Cirella goes to the doctor, and he says, "Doc, you gotta help me. I eat apples, apples come out. I eat bananas, bananas come out."
The doctor says, "It's easy. Eat shit."

Why do bald men cut holes in their pockets?
So they can run their fingers through their hair.

Farmer Petrovich is whipping and slapping his horse when the local minister comes over.

The minister says, "My, Farmer Petrovich, you're certainly giving that animal a beating. You wouldn't do that to your wife, would you?"

The farmer says, "I would if she farted and jumped sideways every time I tried to mount her."

The first hen says, "I sell my eggs for fifty cents a dozen."

The second one says, "Well, my eggs are bigger, and I sell them for fifty-*five* cents a dozen."

The first one says, "So I should bust my ass for a nickel?"

Why do Jews wear yarmulkes?
Because those little propellers are extra.

Ruggles is marooned on a desert island for fourteen years, and then he's finally rescued. They take him to shore, and ask him what he'd like.

He says, "You *know* what I'd like."

They take him to a brothel, he goes upstairs with a girl, they go in a room and they both get undressed. He proceeds to put on a prophylactic, puts cotton in each ear, and finally, puts a clothespin on his nose.

The girl says, "What the hell are you doing?"

He says, "If there's two things in this world that I hate, it's the sound of a woman screaming, and the smell of burning rubber."

What's grosser than your grandfather getting a boner when you're sitting on his lap?
Your grandmother lifting her dress up and saying, "Come on, kids, we're eating out tonight."

Jerkowicz and Snowden are on a camel, traveling through the desert, dying of thirst, and finally come to an oasis. Jerkowicz and Snowden drink up and get refreshed, but the camel refuses to take a drink.

Jerkowicz says, "I've got an idea. You hold the camel's head under water, and I'll suck on his asshole and try to draw some water up into his mouth."

Snowden dunks the camel's head under the water and Jerkowicz starts sucking like mad on his asshole.

After a few minutes, Jerkowicz yells, "Raise his head a little. All I'm getting is mud from the bottom."

How can you tell if an Iranian woman is going steady?
Her boyfriend's initials are carved in the hair on her back.

Little Red Riding Hood's walking along in the woods when the Big, Bad Wolf jumps out and says, "*Grrr* . . . I'm going to fuck you."

She says, "Bull*shit* you're gonna fuck me. You're gonna stick to the script, and you're gonna *eat* me, you hairy bastard. You mangy fucking mongrel, get down there and eat my pussy."

Why does the bride smile walking down the aisle?
Because she knows she's sucked her last cock.

What's the best cure for constipation?
Sit on a block of cheese and swallow a mouse.

Christiano is in bed with a girl and no matter what he does, he just can't seem to get it up.

She says, "Come on, will you? Do *something*."

He says, "Like what?"

She says, "Put your foot in."

He sticks his foot in, and she has a merry old time riding it. A few days later, his foot is swelling up and it's starting to itch, so he goes to the doctor to have it looked at.

The doctor says calmly, "Well, my friend, it seems you have syphilis of the big toe."

Christiano says, "*Syphilis of the big toe?* Jeez, Doc, I bet that's pretty rare."

The doctor says, "Yeah, it's pretty rare. Of course, it's not as rare as the girl who was in here this morning with athlete's cunt."

How about the Polish guy who was jerking off in a restaurant because the sign said, "*First Come, First Served*"?

The Clintons go on a camping trip for their twentieth anniversary.

Mrs. Clinton says, "I gotta take a whizz."

Her husband says, "Well, let's go down to the water."

They go down to a small cliff at the edge of the lake and she hangs her ass over.

Mrs. Clinton says, "Honey, I think I'll pee into that canoe down there."

Her husband looks down and says, "That's no canoe. That's your reflection."

What would you call a guy with no arms,
no legs, and a twelve-inch dick?
Partially handicapped.

I hope you enjoyed this section.
*If you didn't, I'd bet your mom's
pussy is so dry her crabs ride
around in dune buggies.*

Sgt. Pecker

A guy from the deep South comes to New York and he's amazed by the indoor plumbing. He's so intrigued by the way the toilets work that he goes to the sewage disposal plant to check it out. One of the inspectors shows him to the conveyor belt that carries all the bowel movements.

As the piles of shit parade by them, the inspector says, "You can tell by inspection who the assorted feces belong to. See that one? I'm sure it's the turd of a Mexican. See the pieces of taco shell, and the tomato seeds? And this next one is obviously the turd of a Chinaman or a Jap . . . see the fish eyes and the rice in it? And this next one is surely from a queer."

The hick says, "How can you tell?"

The inspector says, "It's dented on one end."

Two missionaries in Africa get caught by a very hostile tribe of cannibals. The cannibals put them in a big pot of water, build a huge fire under it, and leave them there. A few minutes later, one of the missionaries starts to laugh uncontrollably. The other missionary can't believe it.

He says, "What's wrong with you? We're being boiled alive, and they're gonna *eat* us! What could possibly be funny at a time like this?"

The other missionary says, "I just shit in the soup."

What do the gerbils say when the homos
walk into the pet store?
"Arf, arf . . ."

Langon is hired to play his trumpet on the score of a
movie, and he's excited. He's especially thrilled because he
gets to take two long solos. After the sessions, which go
great, Langon can't wait to see the finished product. He asks
the producer where and when he can catch the film. A little
embarrassed, the producer explains that the music is for a
porno flick that will be out in a month, and he tells Langon
where he can go to see it.

A month later, Langon puts his collar up, puts on dark
glasses, and goes to the theater where the picture is playing. He walks in and sits way in the back, next to an elderly
couple who also seem to be disguised and hiding.

The movie starts, and it's the filthiest, most perverse
porno flick ever.

Group sex, S&M, golden showers . . . and then, halfway
through, a dog gets in on the action. Before anyone can
blink an eye, the dog has done all the women in every ori-
fice, and most of the men.

Langon is incredibly embarrassed, and he turns to the
old couple and whispers, "I'm only here for the music."

The woman turns to Langon and whispers back, "We're
here to see our dog."

Harry says to Vinnie, "I sure would like some sex. Thank God I've got some money."

Vinnie says, "I want some, too, but I'll have to go home and get the fifty bucks I lent my wife last week."

Harry says, "What makes you think she'll still have the fifty?"

Vinnie says, "She doesn't drink, and she has her own pussy."

Shire comes home from work and says to his wife, "This is the third night this week I've come home from work and there's no dinner on the table. The *third* night this week there's no dinner on the table."

His wife says, "Oh yeah? Well, we've got four kids. I get 'em up, I dress 'em, I feed 'em breakfast, I get 'em off to school. I do the washing, the cleaning, the ironing, the shopping. I haven't got time to wipe my ass."

He says, "That's *another* thing I want to talk to you about."

Hoagland walks into his house, goes up into his bedroom, and finds his best friend banging his wife.

He freaks out, and says, "Mark, how the hell could you do this? You're supposed to be my *friend*. And in my *own house*. Fucking my . . . Jesus *Christ*, you two, you could at least stop while I'm talking to you."

Melendez walks in to a bar, and says "G-g-gimme a b-b-beer."

The bartender says, "Seems you've got a stuttering problem."

Melendez says, "N-n-no sh-sh-shit."

The bartender says, "I used to stutter, but my wife cured me. She sucked me off three times in a row, and I haven't stuttered since."

Melendez says, "W-w-wow, th-th-that's great to kn-kn-know . . ."

A week later, Melendez walks in to the bar, and says, "G-g-gimme a b-b-beer."

The bartender says, "Why didn't you try what I told you?"

Melendez says, "I d-d-did. It d-d-didn't w-w-work. B-b-but I m-m-must say, you have a r-r-really nice apartment."

Why is a sheep better than a woman?
Because a sheep doesn't care if you fuck her sister.

Dolly Parton and Queen Elizabeth decide to have a popularity contest, so Dolly goes over to England. She walks out on stage, takes off her blouse and her bra, and starts flapping her tits from side to side.

The crowd goes, "We love you, Dolly! We *love* you!"

Queen Elizabeth walks out on stage, sits in a chair, and douches herself.

The crowd goes, "*Yuk!* You *pig!*"

The head judge stands up and says, "Queen Elizabeth wins."

Dolly says, "What do you mean, *Queen Elizabeth wins?*"

He says, "Royal flush beats two of a kind."

Did you hear about the guy who's half
Polish and half Mexican?
*He made a run for the border and forgot
where he was going.*

A Polish guy calls a girl for a date.
She says, "But Stosh, I've got a rag on."
He says, "I'm not that dressed up myself."

How is a condom like a wife?
They spend too much time in your wallet,
and not enough time on your dick.

Rush and Schultz are sitting at the bar when a very pretty girl walks in.

Rush says, "I'd have to give her a nine."

Schultz says, "One."

Another girl, even nicer, walks in.

Rush says, "Whoa . . . nine-five."

Schultz says, "Maybe a two."

Rush says, "Wait one fucking minute. Those two girls are *gorgeous*. All you'd give them on a scale from one to ten is a one or a two?"

Schultz says, "I don't use that stupid one-to-ten scale. I use the Budweiser system."

Rush says, "The *Budweiser system?* What's that?"

Schultz says, "That's how many Clydesdales it would take to rip her off my face."

What would you call shock absorbers
in a compact car?
Passengers.

The Polish maid lets out a piercing shriek and the lady of the house comes running into the bedroom. There's a used prophylactic in the bed.

The lady says, "Mrs. Hornaski, don't you have those in Poland?"

The maid says, "Yeah, but we don't *skin* them."

Why did the Polish proctologist use two fingers?
He wanted to get a second opinion.

A black kid from Bedford-Stuyvesant gets accepted to Harvard. His first day on campus he's walking around kind of lost.

He goes up to another student and says, "Yo, man, where de library at?"

The other student says, "Excuse me? Here at *Harvard,* we don't end a sentence with a *preposition.*"

The black kid says, "Okay. Then where de library at, *motherfucker?*"

What did Cinderella say when she got to the ball?
"Gaghgh."

Dell' Abate goes to buy a train ticket, and the girl selling tickets has an incredible set of jugs.

He says, "Give me two pickets to Titsburgh . . . umm . . . I mean, two tickets to Pittsburgh."

He's really embarrassed.

The guy in line behind him says, "Relax, pal, we all make Freudian slips like that. Just the other day at the breakfast table I meant to say to my wife, 'Please pass the sugar,' but I accidentally said, 'You fucking bitch, you wrecked my life.'"

Did you hear about the hippie who ate
ten prunes with his LSD?
*He figured this was one trip he'd
know where he was going.*

The three stages of what a married couple does in bed:
For the first year, it's fuck watching TV.
For the next five years, it's fuck and watch TV.
And after that, it's watch fucking TV.

How about the Polish guy who thought his wife liked to get fucked in the ear because every time he went to stick his dick in her mouth, she turned her head?

What's the surest sign a man is in love?
When he divorces his wife.

A salesman knocks on Farmer Gossman's door, and when he gets no answer, he walks around the back of the house. There's Farmer Gossman, with a cow's tail lifted up, planting a huge wet kiss on the cow's asshole.

The salesman says, "Man, are you queer or *what?*"

Farmer Gossman says, "No. I've got chapped lips, and it keeps me from lickin' em."

Why are all the blacks moving to Detroit?
Because they heard there are no jobs there.

Messina meets a native girl in Hawaii, and they go out in the bushes to fool around. They're just getting down to it when she stands up, starts dancing, and then starts to take a leak.

He says, "What are you doing?"

She says, "It's just the rain of the islands."

They get back to it, they're going hot and heavy, when she suddenly stands up, starts dancing again, and then lets out a whopping fart.

Messina says, "*Now* what's going on?"

She says, "It's just the wind of the islands."

He gets up and walks away.

She yells, "Where are you going?"

He says, "I can't fuck in this climate."

How did the gynecologist know his patient was horny?
He read her lips.

Remember . . . if it smells like fish, it's a dish.

If it smells like cologne, leave it alone.

Trish goes into a bar and she says, "Bartender, give me a triple Jack Daniels."

He gives her a triple Jack Daniels, and she belts it down. She has five more in a row, belts them all down, passes out dead drunk, and everybody in the bar fucks her.

The next night, she walks into the bar, and says, "Bartender, give me a triple Jack Daniels."

He gives her a triple Jack Daniels, and she belts it down. She has five more in a row, belts them all down, passes out dead drunk, and everybody in the bar fucks her again.

The next night, she walks into the bar and says, "Bartender, give me a triple Tequila."

He says, "I thought you drank Jack Daniels."

She says, "Not any more. Jack Daniels makes my pussy sore."

A Jew gets mugged.

The crook says, "Give me your money or I'll cut your balls off."

The Jew says "Can I have a minute to think it over?"

Sloman gets in a big barroom brawl and his jaw gets smashed up so badly that they have to wire it shut. So for a few weeks he has to be fed through his butt.

After a couple days, he mumbles through his wired-up jaw to the nurse, "Nurse, I can't stand it. I gotta have a cup of coffee. I *gotta* have a cup of coffee."

So the nurse gets a tube, sticks it up his ass, puts a funnel in the tube, and pours in the coffee.

Sloman starts waggling around, going "Unh! *Unh!*"

She says, "Is it too hot?"

He says, "No! It's too *sweet!*"

Mrs. Prezocki walks into a sex store and says to the salesman, "Where are the dildos?"

The clerk says, "On the wall over there . . . "

She looks and then points and says, "I want one of the red ones."

The salesman says, "No, lady. The dildos are the ones *next* to the fire extinguisher."

Fallon goes into an alley with a hooker, starts to go down on her, and there's peas and carrots and chewed meat in there.

He says, "Lady, are you *sick?*"

She says, "No, but I think the guy before you might have been."

What does an eight-hundred-and-fifty-pound
gerbil do for kicks?
He shoves gay guys up his ass.

Why does it take longer to build a
snowwoman than a snowman?
Because you have to hollow out the head.

I hope you enjoyed this section.
*If you didn't, I hope your next
shit is square.*

Kiss
the Pickle

A little old lady walks into a butcher shop, walks over to where the chickens are hanging, lifts up a chicken's wing, and sniffs under it. She lifts up another wing and sniffs under it. She lifts up a leg and sniffs under it.

The butcher yells over, "Hey, lady . . . you think *you* could pass that test?"

She says, "I want a nice Long Island duckling."

He says, "Okay, lady," and he brings out a duckling.

She unwraps it, sticks her finger in its rear end, pulls it out, and sniffs it.

She says, "Hey! What are you trying to do? This duckling's not from Long Island. This duckling is from Pennsyl*vania.*"

The butcher says, "Hang on, lady."

He brings out another duck.

She unwraps its, sticks her finger in its rear end, pulls it out, and sniffs it.

She says, "Wait just a minute. This duckling is not from Long Island. This duckling is from *upstate* New York."

He says, "Hang on, lady."

He brings out another duck.

She unwraps it, puts her finger in its rear end, and wiggles it around a little . . .

She pulls it out, sniffs it, and says, "Now that's a nice Long Island duckling. I'll take it. You can wrap it up. Gee, you're certainly a nice young fella. You must be new around here. Where'd you say you're from?"

He pulls down his pants, turns around, bends over, and says, "You tell me."

Jackie "The Joke Man" Martling's

Did you hear about the Polish airliner
that crashed in a graveyard?
So far, they've recovered five thousand bodies.

Why aren't there any Puerto
Ricans on *Star Trek*?
*Because they're not going to work
in the future, either.*

A black guy has stomach cramps so he goes to a black
doctor.

The doctor examines him, and says, "Well, my friend,
you bowels is locked."

He says, "But, Doc, I gots diarrhea."

The doctor says, "Then they's locked *open*."

What's the difference between
outlaws and in-laws?
Outlaws are *wanted*.

Pippin comes home from a party and yells to his wife, "Honey, I want to show you something."

She comes into the living room, and Pippin is standing there with a beautiful gold trophy.

She says, "Where did you get that?"

He says, "I won it in a big dick contest."

She says, "You mean to tell me that you pulled that big hairy thing out of your pants in front of a group of strangers again?"

Pippin says, "Just enough to win."

A middle-aged lady's got a bad backache, so she goes to the doctor. After he examines her, he tells her to go home, take a hot bath, and then lie on her bed naked and pull her legs up over her head.

She goes home and does it. She's lying on top of her bed stark naked, with her knees back by her ears, when her husband walks in from work.

He says, "For Christ's sakes, Linda, comb your hair and put in your teeth. You look more like your mother every day."

What did one gay sperm say to
the other gay sperm?
*"How are we supposed to find an
egg in all this shit?"*

Did you hear about the dyslexic rabbi?
He walks around saying, "Yo."

God wants to go on a vacation, and he doesn't know where to go.

One of the angels says, "God, why don't you go down to Earth?"

God says, "Nah. I mean, Earth's got a pretty good atmosphere, but I went there two thousand years ago and banged some Jewish girl, and they're still talking about it."

Fred and Al ride a camel to a football game, and leave it in the parking lot. After the game, they agree that it'll be hard to find the camel with the parking lot so crowded, so they have a few beers and wait a while. Finally, they go to the parking lot, and it's empty except for the camel.

Just before they get on, Fred says, "Hold it, Al, I'm gonna make sure this is ours."

He walks around behind it, lifts up the camel's tail, and says, "This ain't it. It ain't ours."

Al says, "How do you know?"

Fred says, "When we were riding in, I heard the guy at the gate say, 'Look at the two assholes on that camel.'"

What's the smartest thing that ever came
out of a woman's mouth?
Einstein's cock.

How do you know when you're really stoned on pot?
*You're sitting there picking away at the
holiday turkey and it's still frozen.*

Why did the Polish guy slide down the banister?
He was out of toilet paper.

How do you make a dog go "meow"?
Put him in a deep freeze for a few days . . .
then push him through a buzz saw . . .
meeooww . . .

A Polish girl is hitchhiking and gets picked up by a trucker. She gets in, and the first thing she notices is his fancy CB setup.

She says, "Wow, what a nice radio."

He says, "I can call anywhere in the world with that."

She says, "Really? I'd do anything to talk to my mother home in Poland . . ."

He says, "Oh, yeah?" and takes out his huge cock.

She grabs it, leans down, and says, "Hello, Ma?"

How can you tell when a girl is really horny?
She sits on your hand and it feels like
there's a horse eating out of your palm.

Sidor is at a banquet and keeps complaining that his false teeth are hurting him.

The guy sitting to his left reaches into his pocket and pulls out a set of dentures, hands them to Sidor, and says, "Try these."

Sidor tries them, and says, "Thanks anyway, but they're too tight."

The guy pulls out another set and hands them to Sidor. They fit perfectly, so Sidor wears them for the entire night.

At the end of the banquet, Sidor hands them back to the guy and says, "They fit me perfectly. Are you a dentist?"

The guy says, "No. An undertaker."

What's the definition of safe sex in West Virginia?
Branding the sheep that kick.

Two gay guys are on a picnic, and the first guy says, "I have to take a dumpski," and he walks into the woods to do it.

A few minutes later, the other guy hears the first guy whimpering, "*Boo-hoo!* I had a miscarriage. I had a *miscarriage.*"

He goes running into the woods to see what's going on.

When he gets there, the first guy is still crying, "*Boo-hoo!* I had a miscarriage. I had a *miscarriage.*"

He looks down and says, "Don't be *silly.* You didn't have a *miscarriage.* You had diarrhea on a frog."

Why are turds tapered at the end?
So your asshole won't slam shut.

Did you hear about the two gays whose
last wish was to be buried together?
*The mortician cremated them and
put them in a fruit jar.*

Parenteau's got a big fat wife. She gets out of the shower, sits on the pot, and gets stuck, so he calls the plumber. Then he realizes that she's sitting there naked, and he can't have that, so he takes his bowler derby and puts it on her lap to cover up home base.

The plumber shows up, takes one look, and he says, "Listen, Mac, I think I can save your wife, but the guy in the hat's a goner."

Where does an Irish family go on vacation?
To a different bar.

When do you know you've got a really small cock?
You put it in a girl's hand and she says,
"You know I don't get high."

How do you paralyze a woman
from the waist down?
Marry her.

Bates walks into the doctor's office with a golf club sticking out of his ass.

The doctor says, "What the hell happened to you?"

Bates says, "I sliced a shot into a cow pasture. We spent a half hour looking for my ball when my wife called me over to see it deeply imbedded in a pile of cow shit. I wasn't thinking and I said, 'Looks like your hole.'"

A married couple goes to a masquerade party dressed as a cow. He's the front, she's the back. The party gets a little boring, so they decide to stay in their costume and go for a walk.

As they're going across a pasture, they hear, *Snort! Snort!*

The wife says, "Bobby! *Bobby!* There's a *bull* over there and I think he's gonna charge! What are we gonna do?"

The husband says, "Well, I'm gonna eat some grass . . . you better brace yourself."

What do two lesbians do when
they're both menstruating?
Fingerpaint.

Two gay guys get married, and they want to have a baby, so they ask a girl to let them both make love to her, and then have the baby for them. And she agrees, because if she didn't, this joke would stop right here. Nine months later, they're in the maternity ward, and all of the babies are kicking and screaming except for one.

One of the gay guys says to the nurse, "Nurse, oh, nurse, which is *our* child?"

Of course, she's pretty annoyed at the whole situation.

She says, "The one that's quiet."

The gay guy says, "See? So calm and peaceful."

She says, "Yeah? Wait 'til I take the pacifier out of his ass."

What would you call an Italian slum?
A spaghetto.

Woodbury calls the undertaker and says, "You're gonna have to bury my wife."

The undertaker says, "Bury your wife? I buried your wife two years ago."

Woodbury says, "You don't understand, I got married again."

The undertaker says, "Oh, I didn't know that. Congratulations."

A couple's in bed, and the guy says, "How about it?"

She says, "Not tonight, I have to go to the gynecologist tomorrow and I want to be fresh."

The guy thinks a second and says, "You're not going to the *dentist,* are you?"

Why was it easy to pick out
George Washington's mistresses?
They all had splinters in their tits.

The doctor walks up to Legman in the hospital and says, "I'm sorry, but your wife is very weak. I doubt that she'll make it to the morning. Try to comfort her as best you can."

Legman goes into her room, and says, "Dear, the doctor says things are bleak. Is there anything I can do to comfort you in your last hours?"

She says, "Well, all these years we've been married, I'd always wished that one day you'd fuck me in the ass, but you never have. Would you please do that?"

Legman is astounded, but it's her last request, so he figures he should do whatever she desires. Face it, he's thrilled. So, he rolls her over, lifts her nightie, and proceeds to skewer her manure. Really stirs her lunch for her, boffs her in the potty spot for hours.

The next morning the doctor looks in on her, and he can't believe it. She's made an incredible rally, and is rapidly regaining her strength and her health. By noon, she's up and walking. The doctor is flabbergasted.

He pulls Legman out into the hall and says, "My God, man, she's like *new*. She's going to live to be a hundred and twenty. What the hell did you *do* in there?"

Legman is a little embarrassed by the whole situation, and he says, "Well, Doc, I . . . I just . . . I just fucked her in the ass for a while."

The doctor starts to cry uncontrollably.

Legman says, "Doc, what's wrong?"

The doctor says, "I could have saved my father, Eleanor Roosevelt . . ."

What's brown and hides in the attic?
The diarrhea of Anne Frank.

Louis and Jim are sitting on a dock fishing. Louis reaches into his bait box, takes out a piece of bait, *sniffs!* it, puts it on the hook, throws in his line, and pulls out a fish. He reaches into his bait box, takes out a piece of bait, *sniffs!* it, puts it on the hook, throws in his line, and pulls out a fish.

After a while Jim says, "Wait one fucking minute. You reach into your bait box, take out a piece of bait, *sniff!* it, put it on your hook, throw in your line, and pull out a fish, fish after fish. I'm sitting here right next to you, and I haven't even got a friggin' *nibble.* What the hell are you using for bait?"

Louis says, "Well, I'm a little embarrassed. I've got a friend who's an undertaker, and he sells me pussies to use for bait. I put 'em on the hook, and the fish can't resist 'em."

Jim says, "I can understand that. But why do you *sniff* 'em?"

Louis says, "Well, he's a low-life bastard, and every once in a while he slips in a few assholes."

Did you hear about the Mexican midget who committed suicide?
He hung himself from his rearview mirror.

Why did the shit cross the road?
The chicken forgot to wipe her ass.

Why don't elephants use tampons?
You wouldn't use them either, if you had to put them in with your nose.

I hope you enjoyed this section. *If you didn't, I hope the next time you jump on a bicycle it doesn't have a seat.*

What Did You Expect?

Bartlett is checking out of a hotel when suddenly he has to take a shit real bad. The bathroom door in his room is stuck shut, so he bolts down to use the lobby men's room, but all of the stalls are occupied, so he runs back up to his room, and in desperation, he drops his pants, uproots a plant, and takes a shit in the pot.

Then he puts the plant back in the pot and leaves.

Two weeks later, he gets a postcard from the hotel that says, "Dear Mr. Bartlett, All is forgiven. Just tell us . . . where is it?"

We're out on the Great Plains in the mid-1800s with the legendary Indian hunter, Running Sore. And he's with his protégé, Licking Red Beaver. Suddenly, Running Sore *hushes* Licking Red Beaver. He gets down on all fours . . . because obviously he *trusts* Licking Red Beaver . . . and he puts one ear to the ground.

He says, "Buffalo come."

Licking Red Beaver says, "How you know?"

He says, "Stuck to my cheek."

What do you get when you cross
Van Gogh with a Mexican?
*A bullfighter who cuts off his own ear and
throws it to the crowd.*

A doctor makes a routine phone call to one of his elderly patients, and he says, "How are you feeling, Mr. Schwartz?"

He says, "I feel fine, Doc, but you know, it's the damnedest thing. Every night when I get up to pee, and I open up the bathroom door, the light goes on for me automatically."

The doctor is worried that the old guy is getting a little senile, so he calls the guy's son, and the son's wife answers. He says, "Mrs. Schwartz, I'm a little concerned about your father-in-law. It seems that when he gets up in the middle of the night to urinate, and opens the bathroom door, he claims the light goes on automatically, and I . . ."

She yells, "Ernie! Pop's pissing in the refrigerator again!"

Mrs. Benson says to the funeral director, just before her husband's wake, "You know, Charlie looks great, but I'm so worried about his toupee sliding down. I know it would just break his heart if his toupee slid down."

The mortician says, "Don't worry about a thing, lady."

Two days later, the funeral's over, and Mrs. Benson says to the mortician, "Charlie's toupee stayed right in place. I can't thank you enough. What'd you do?"

He says, "I stapled it on."

Did you hear the boys from West Virginia
have found a new use for sheep?
They get wool from them.

Did you hear about the promiscuous high school girl?
While everyone else was dissecting frogs,
she was opening flies.

An old guy's sitting on a bus when a punk rocker gets on. The punk rocker's hair is red, yellow, blue, and orange, he's wearing feather earrings, and he sees the guy staring at him.

He says, "What's the matter, old man? Didn't you ever do anything wild?"

The guy says, "Yeah. One time I fucked a parrot. I thought maybe you were my kid."

What would you call a girl who eats
her mother and her father?
An orphan.

Iacovelli walks into a bar and has a couple of beers. He goes to take a piss, and while he's pissing, he looks over and sees a guy bending over to wash his hands in the sink. While he's bending over, another guy comes up from behind and starts fucking him in the ass. Then *another* guy comes up behind *him* and starts fucking *him* in the ass. Iacovelli can't believe it.

He goes back out to the bartender and says, "What's going on? A guy was washing his hands in the sink, another guy comes up from behind and starts fucking him in the ass, then *another* guy comes up behind *him* and starts fucking *him* in the ass."

The bartender says, "Was the guy in the middle wearing an orange shirt?"

Iacovelli says, "Yeah."

The bartender says, "That's Bob. He's lucky in cards, too."

What did the brown gerbil say to the white gerbil?
"You must be new around here."

Dirty Johnny's playing with Loose Lisa, and he says to her, "You know, Lisa, I'd really like to get in your pants."

She says, "Why, John?"

He says, "Because I just shit in mine."

What's the one thing you can do to a Jewish girl's
asshole to make her squeal with delight?
Give him a raise.

The doctor says, "Schlatter, you've got sugar in your
urine."

The next morning, Schlatter pees on his cornflakes.

Beno and Puscas are bombed, watching the St. Patrick's
Day parade, when one of them drops his lit cigarette into a
damp mattress that's been left out on the sidewalk. The
mattress starts to smoulder just as the blue-hair brigade,
the ladies' auxiliary, is passing by.

Beno takes a whiff, turns to Puscas, and says, "*Man . . .
you think maybe they're marching these ladies too fast?*"

What does a perverted parrot say?
"Polly want a rim job."

Minervini goes into a whorehouse, goes upstairs with a girl, takes off his pants, and he's got a two-foot cock.

She says, "Bullshit. You're not putting that thing in *me*. I'll *kiss* it."

He says, "Fuck *that*. I can do that my*self*."

Did you hear about the couple
that "ninety-sixed"?
*After they sixty-nined, they rolled over
and shit in each other's hair.*

Luke says to his Pa, "Pa, what's fuckin'?"

Pa calls Ma over, bends her over a rain barrel, lifts up her skirt, pulls down her drawers, points, and says to Luke, "See that hole in Ma? Well, watch me."

He pulls down his pants and starts fucking her from behind.

As Pa is pumping Ma, Luke's brother Zeke comes running over and says, "Luke, we gotta help Ma, Pa's beatin' her up."

Luke says, "No, Pa's fuckin'."

Zeke says, "What's fuckin'?"

Luke yanks down his pants, points, and says, "See that hole in Pa? Well, watch me."

What's brown and full of holes?
Swiss shit.

How do you make Polish stucco?
You paint over the boogers.

Hawthorne buys a parrot, and the first night he has it, he brings home a girl, and the parrot screeches, "He's gonna try to fuck you! He's gonna try to fuck you!"

After he takes her home, he says to the parrot, "You pull that shit again, I'll slash your throat and throw you in the toilet."

The next night, he brings home a girl, and the parrot screeches, "He's gonna try to fuck you! He's gonna try to fuck you!"

Hawthorne grabs the parrot, slashes his throat, and throws him in the toilet. He goes back to the girl and it turns out she's having her period, so she excuses herself to go yank out her tampon.

She's sitting on the bowl after she yanks it out, when she hears, "I'm gonna live! I'm gonna live!"

She gets up and sees the parrot in the bowl with his neck sliced open.

She says, "What do you mean, 'You're gonna live'?"

The parrot points to her bloody snatch and says, "If you can live with a gash like *that,* I can live with a gash like *this!*"

Jackie "The Joke Man" Martling's

How do you know when you've got really bad gas?
You fart in the tub and the bubbles sink.

When do you know you're really lonely?
Your own tongue starts to feel good in your mouth.

How do you make a cat go "woof"?
*You cover it with gasoline, and throw on a match . . .
woof . . .*

Life isn't fair. They'll put Bibles in motel rooms,
but you'll never get a vibrating pew.

Why did the French horn player's
wife get a divorce?
*Because every time he kissed her
he stuck his hand in her ass.*

Fox and Clarke are sitting at a bar.

Fox says, "You ever have anal sex?"

Clarke says, "Yeah."

Fox says, "With who?"

Clarke says, "My wife."

Fox says, "Do you like it?"

Clarke says, "Nah, not really."

Fox says, "Does your wife like it?"

Clarke says, "Not really."

Fox says, "So you hardly ever do it?"

Clarke says, "Are you kidding? We do it almost every night."

Fox says, "*You* don't like it, and your *wife* doesn't like it. Why the hell do you do it?"

Clarke says, "The kids get a big kick out of it."

How do you make five pounds
of fat look pretty?
Put a nipple on the end.

Jackie "The Joke Man" Martling's

DiNapoli comes home from work and finds his new bride sliding down the banister.

He says, "What are you doing?"

She says, "Warming up your dinner."

The farmer sends his daughter to the meat market for pig's feet, forgetting that the town has a new butcher who doesn't speak any English. Sure enough, his daughter comes home with the pig's feet.

The farmer says, "How did you tell him you wanted pig's feet?"

She says, "I just pointed to my feet and grunted like a pig."

The farmer says, "Well, I'm certainly glad I didn't send you for a ham."

Your wife is barking at the front door,
and your dog is barking at the back door.
Who do you let in?
The dog . . . because he stops barking
after you let him in.

Why do doctors spank newborn babies?
To knock the dicks off the stupid ones.

Pinkerton is drunk and he goes up into a room with a big fat hooker. She takes off her clothes, jumps on the bed, lies on her back, and spreads her legs.

He takes a look and says, "What am I doing in this lane? I don't have exact change."

A lady says to her doctor, "My husband has been complaining that my vagina has an odor, but I bent over and took a whiff, and I don't smell anything."

The doctor examines her, and then says, "You need an operation."

She says, "On my vagina?"

He says, "No. On your nose."

What's the difference between a girl and a toilet?
A toilet doesn't want to cuddle after you drop a load in it.

Hammond is walking up to a doctor's office when a nun comes running out screaming.

Hammond walks in and says, "What's with the nun?"

The doctor says, "I just told her that she's pregnant."

Hammond says, "The nun is *pregnant?*"

The doctor says, "No, but it certainly cured her hiccups."

Ferrentino wakes up one morning with a terrible hangover, and realizes he's in a motel room. He looks down at the foot of the bed, and there she is. *Ooo.* Very ugly. A girl that's so ugly they should retire the letters of her name from the alphabet. She's looking at him, and she's in love.

She says, "What are we gonna name it?"

Ferrentino picks up the rubber he used the night before, ties a knot in it, twirls it around, tosses it out the window, and says, "If he gets out of *this* one, we'll call him Hou*dini.*"

What's the best thing about Alzheimer's disease?
You can hide your own Easter eggs.

When do you know your girlfriend is
spending too much time on your face?
*There's an imprint of her
asshole on your chin.*

Raney is in a locker room when he sees a guy with a cork in his ass.

He says to him, "Hey, I know it's none of my business, but why is there a cork in your ass?"

The guy says, "Well, I was walking in the woods when I tripped over a lamp. This thing came out and said, '*Ugh!* Me Tonto, Indian genie. Can grant-um you one wish.' And I said, 'No shit.'"

Planncton goes into the tiny, dingy little office of Stanley Schwartz, a disreputable, snaky, low-life show business booking agent, and says, "I want you to look at an act."

Stanley Schartz says, "Okay, step out into the hall."

They walk out into the hall, and Stanley Schwartz says to Planncton, "Okay, let's see what you've got."

Planncton gets totally naked, and then shits on the floor. As he's finishing a nice pile, his sister comes around the corner and dives into the muck. He starts undressing her as his father and brother, both naked, come around the corner with huge erections, pulling on them madly. They both piss on the sister and take shits themselves, and then they sing a little song and do a little dance in the mess. Then the mother appears in drag, and starts sucking off the brother and waddling in the excretion as the sister barfs and the father leads them in a little song and a little dance.

Then they all meet heads together in the crap, and come up dripping and smiling with a loud, "Hooray!"

Planncton says to Stanley Schwartz, "What do you think?"

Stanley Schwartz says, "It's very different. What do you call yourselves?"

Planncton says, "The Aristocrats."

I hope you enjoyed this book. *If you didn't, why don't you go piss into a fan? And while you're at it, stand too close..*